MYTHOLOGY OF
THE CELTS

MYTHOLOGY OF
THE CELTS

MYTHS AND LEGENDS OF THE CELTIC WORLD

ARTHUR COTTERELL

southwater

This edition is published by Southwater

Southwater is an imprint of Anness Publishing Ltd
Hermes House, 88–89 Blackfriars Road, London SE1 8HA
tel. 020 7401 2077; fax 020 7633 9499
www.southwaterbooks.com; info@anness.com

© Anness Publishing Ltd 1997, 2003

This edition distributed in the UK by The Manning
Partnership Ltd, 6 The Old Dairy, Melcombe Road,
Bath BA2 3LR;
tel. 01225 478 444; fax 01225 478 440;
sales@manning-partnership.co.uk

This edition distributed in the USA and Canada by National
Book Network, 4501 Forbes Boulevard,
Suite 200, Lanham, MD 20706;
tel. 301 459 3366; fax 301 429 5746; www.nbnbooks.com

This edition distributed in Australia by
Pan Macmillan Australia, Level 18, St Martins Tower,
31 Market St, Sydney, NSW 2000;
tel. 1300 135 113; fax 1300 135 103;
customer.service@macmillan.com.au

This edition distributed in New Zealand by
The Five Mile Press (NZ) Ltd, PO Box 33–1071 Takapuna,
Unit 11/101–111 Diana Drive, Glenfield, Auckland 10;
tel. (09) 444 4144; fax (09) 444 4518;
fivemilenz@xtra.co.nz

A CIP catalogue record for this book is available from
the British Library.

Publisher: Joanna Lorenz
Editorial Manager: Helen Sudell
Project Editor: Belinda Wilkinson
Designer: Nigel Soper, Millions Design
Illustrators: James Alexander, Nick Beale,
Glenn Steward
Previously published as *Celtic Mythology*

10 9 8 7 6 5 4 3 2 1

Page One: The Gundestrup Cauldron *c.* 100BC
Frontispiece: *Etain, Helen, Medband and Fand* by Harry Clarke
This page: *Parzival* by Martin Wiegand

Author's Note

The entries in this encyclopedia are all listed alphabetically.
Where more than one name exists for a character the entry
is listed under the name used in the original country of
origin for that particular myth. Names in italic capital letters
indicate that that name has an individual entry. Special
feature spreads examine specific mythological themes in
more detail. If a character is included in a special feature
spread it is noted at the end of their individual entry.

CONTENTS

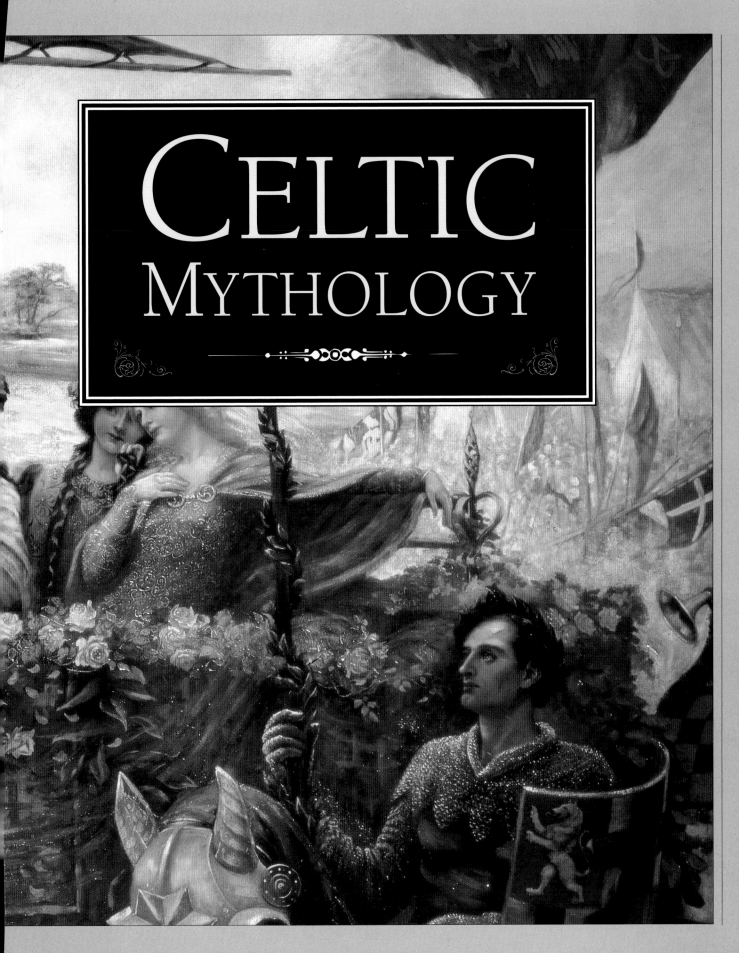

CELTIC
MYTHOLOGY

INTRODUCTION

TODAY PEOPLE OF CELTIC DESCENT IN Europe are concentrated on its western shores. They live chiefly in Brittany, Cornwall, Wales, Scotland, the Isle of Man and Ireland. At one time, however, the Celts were spread over a large part of the Continent, and in 278 BC one roving band even penetrated as far east as Asia Minor, where they gave their name to Galatia. Until the rise of Roman power, the Celts were a force to be reckoned with. Rome itself had been sacked by them in 385 BC, a historical fact not forgotten by the legionaries who gave Julius Caesar victory between 59 and 49 BC over the Celtic tribes living in Gaul, present-day France. Although largely incorporated into the Roman Empire, the Celts continued to worship their own gods and goddesses right up to the time of the official adoption by the Romans of the Christian faith. Then their religion and mythology waned in importance, except where people remembered tales about the Celtic gods and heroes of the past. Even in distant Ireland, an island that was never under Roman control, the influence of Christianity was soon felt. But here conversion did not mean the wholesale destruction of the Celtic heritage, for monks took great care from the fifth century onwards to write down the ancient sagas.

To this remarkable effort of preservation we owe almost our entire knowledge of Celtic mythology. For except in Wales, where a small group of stories was recorded, nothing else was ever committed to writing. The Celts always distrusted script and preferred to rely on speech and properly trained memories.

In Ireland the poet was held in particular esteem. Possibly because there was a clear distinction there between druid and poet in pre-Christian times. The newly-founded monasteries could therefore undertake the work of recording the ancient texts without any fear of paganism. It seems that poets went on reciting the sagas long after St Patrick converted the Irish and cleared the country of snakes, because these tales were seen as entertainment. Irish folklore insists, however, that they kept something of their magic, since the Devil could never enter a house where the exploits of the heroes were being sung.

BRANWEN was a classic Celtic heroine who remained calm and dignified under pressure. A falsely slandered wife, she was forced to suffer unjustly, until rescued by her brother, Bran the Blessed. (BRANWEN BY G SHERRINGHAM, CANVAS, C. 1920.)

Irish myths nearly always include fighting, though the combat is undertaken more often by heroes than by gods. The fearless warrior Cuchulainn, the lone defender of Ulster during the invasion of forces raised by Queen Medb of Connacht, is very much the ideal. He was chosen as the Irish champion after a beheading contest with the water giant Uath. No other man had courage enough to receive the giant's return blow. Yet Cuchalainn, "the Hound of Culann", enjoyed but a brief life; his refusal to return the affections of Morrigan, the goddess of slaughter, sealed his fate. Not even the intervention of his father Lugh, the sun god, could save him.

The apparently endless conflict appears less terrible when it is recalled how the Celts believed in reincarnation. Their otherworld, unlike the Greek or Roman underworld, was not a dismal abode of the dead. Rather it was a paradise in which souls rested prior to their rebirth in the world. The warrior-poet Oisin, son of the Fenian leader Finn MacCool, spent three hundred years there before returning to Ireland. Oisin was warned that he would never be able to go back to the underworld if he dismounted from a magic steed. When the saddle slipped and he fell to the ground, Oisin was immediately changed from a handsome youth into a blind, grey-haired, withered old man. Only St Patrick is said to have bothered to listen to his fantastic story as it was being written down.

The interest of St Patrick in the adventures of Oisin and, indeed in the exploits of many other heroes of old, is obviously a later embellishment, but it does indicate a degree of tolerance not readily found elsewhere in Christian Europe. Yet saints in Ireland could curse as well as anyone else when the occasion demanded. For instance, the troublesome King Suibhne Geilt was cursed by St Ronan for his violence towards the faith, and

HEROIC combat was a feature of Celtic culture and myth. Champions, such as Cuchulainn, fought to the death, often defending their clan alone. The warriors here wear helmets with boar and raven motifs; symbols of ferocity and death. (GUNDESTRUP CAULDRON, GILDED SILVER, C. 100 BC.)

spent the rest of his life with the characteristics of a bird, leaping from tree to tree and eating at nights nothing but watercress.

In late Celtic mythology, especially the Arthurian myths, Christianity has become a central element. The quest for the Grail is the most obvious example. Although similar to a Celtic magic cauldron, this holy vessel was the cup used at the Last Supper and, at the Crucifixion, the one that received the blood which flowed from the spear thrust in Christ's side. It was brought to Britain by Joseph of Arimathea, but was later lost and its quest preoccupied King Arthur's knights. Only Sir Galahad was pure enough to be granted a full vision of the Grail, which he took as "Our Lord's body between his hands".

Whether or not Arthur was a historical

MERLIN AND NIMUE represent opposite poles of the Celtic otherworld. Merlin, in the tradition of Celtic druids, guided his king, Arthur, with wisdom and foresight; while Nimue, his enchantress, symbolized the threatening powers of the otherworld. (THE BEGUILING OF MERLIN BY E BURNE JONES, CANVAS, C. 1870–74.)

figure is still uncertain. It is quite likely that he may have been a successful warlord in the confused and violent period following the withdrawal of the Roman legions from Britain around 410 AD. That his myth blames the ultimate victory won by the Anglo-Saxon invaders on civil strife perhaps reflects a kernel of truth. The Celtic peoples were notorious for only rarely combining against an external, common foe, so deep-rooted were their own bitter quarrels. Thus British chivalry came to an end with King Arthur's disastrous battle against his nephew Modred near Salisbury. Hardly a knight survived and the King himself was badly wounded. His departure to Avalon, accompanied by three mysterious ladies, gave rise to the idea of his undeath. In an otherworld, it was believed, King Arthur lingered, awaiting reincarnation as a national saviour.

ARTHUR and his Christian Fellowship of Knights probably derived from the earlier Welsh warlord Arthur, who journeyed to the otherworld with his warband in search of a wondrous cauldron. Here, the Knights of the Round Table experience the Grail vision for the first time, amid divine light and splendour. (MANUSCRIPT ILLUSTRATION, C. 1470.)

CALEDONIA

● LINDISFARNE

TORY ISLAND

ULSTER

EMAIN MACHA

MEATH

ISLE OF MAN

IRELAND

BRIGANTES

PARISI

KELLS
●

CONNAUGHT

R. BOYNE

NEW GRANGE
●

● SETANTII

TARA ●

● DUBLIN

R. SHANNON

R. LIFFEY

ANGLESEY

BRITAIN

LEINSTER

IRISH SEA

R. SEVERN

MUNSTER

DYFED

● CORK

● CAMULOS

● LONDINIUM

STONEHENGE
⊓⊓

GLASTONBURY ●

● SALISBURY

● TINTAGEL

ABARTA, which probably means "doer of deeds", was, in Irish mythology, a mischievous god. He was one of the *TUATHA DE DANANN*, who ruled Ireland until they were overcome by the Milesians, war-like invaders from Spain. Driven underground, Abarta and his kin appear in the Irish sagas more like heroic mortals than gods, although in the tale of his trick on the Fenian warriors there remains a strong trace of his original divinity.

Abarta offered himself as a servant to *FINN MACCOOL*, one of the foremost Irish heroes, and hereditary leader of the *FIANNA*. Abarta tried to serve Finn MacCool shortly after the hero had succeeded his father as leader of the band. As a gesture of goodwill, tricky Abarta presented the Fianna with a wild, grey horse. Only after great effort did the warriors manage to get a bridle on the animal, and then it refused to move even one hoof when mounted. It was not until fourteen warriors had climbed on its powerful back that it would stir at all. Once Abarta had mounted behind them, it broke immediately into a gallop, even pulling along a fifteenth warrior who was unable to let go of the horse's tail. Abarta took them to the otherworld, for that was the reason for his appearance on earth. This wonderful land was thought by the Celts to be the home of the gods and goddesses, and the place where souls briefly rested before rebirth. The rest of the Fianna, or Fenians, acquired a magic ship to give chase to Abarta's steed. The best tracker among them was Finn MacCool's assistant Foltor. He succeeded in navigating a course to the otherworld for the rescue expedition. There Abarta was compelled to release the prisoners as well as to run back to Ireland himself holding on to the horse's tail. Honour being satisfied, the Fenians agreed to a peace with Abarta.

AILILL, who was the brother of Eochaidh, a High King of Ireland,

AINE, Irish goddess of love and fertility, was worshipped on Midsummer Eve by the local people who lit up her hill with torches. When some girls stayed late one night, Aine appeared among them and revealed the hill to be alive with fairies, which were only visible through her magic ring.
(ILLUSTRATION BY NICK BEALE, 1995.)

fell in love with his brother's wife, *ETAIN*, who was actually a goddess, one of the *TUATHA DE DANANN*. Etain had been the second wife of the proud and handsome god *MIDIR*, who lived under a mound in the middle of Ireland. She had been reborn as a human as punishment for her great jealousy of Midir's first wife, Fuamnach. When High King Eochaidh was looking for a bride himself, he heard reports that described Etain as the fairest maiden in Ireland. So he brought the beautiful former goddess back to his palace at Tara, the capital. There Eochaidh and Etain enjoyed a happy married life. Ailill, however, gradually succumbed to a terrible wasting disease because of his unrequited passion for the new queen.

Etain was steadfast in her love for Eochaidh, but she also

AMAETHON, though the fruitful rustic god of agriculture, was not always helpful. It was Amaethon that robbed Arawn, thereby provoking the Battle of Trees, and who refused to help hard-pressed Culhwch to plough, sow and reap a hill in a day – a task in his quest to win Olwen.
(ILLUSTRATION BY NICK BEALE, 1995.)

felt sorry for ailing Ailill and eventually promised to satisfy his desire as the only means of saving his life. It was arranged that they should meet secretly in a house outside Tara. However, Ailill never came because he fell into an enchanted sleep.

AILILL MAC MATA, according to some versions of the myth, was the king of Connacht and husband of the warrior-queen *MEDB*. He is generally portrayed as a rather weak character who was entirely under the influence of Medb. It was due to her taunting that he agreed to go to war with Ulster over the Brown Bull of Cuailgne. Ailill finally met his death at the hands of *CONALL*, who killed him in revenge for the death of *FERGUS MAC ROTH*.

AINE was the Irish goddess of love and fertility. She was the daughter of Eogabail, who was the foster son of the Manx sea god *MANANNAN MAC LIR*. Her main responsibilty was to encourage human love, although one mortal lover of hers, King Aillil Olom of Munster, paid for his passionate audacity with his life. When he

attempted to force himself upon Aine and rape her, she slew him with her magic.

Aine's worship was always associated in Ireland with agriculture, because, as a goddess of fertility, she had command over crops and animals. Even as late as the last century, celebrations were still held in her honour on Midsummer Eve at Knockainy, or "Aine's hill", in County Kerry.

AMAETHON (whose name means "labourer" or "ploughman") was the god of agriculture and the son of the Welsh goddess DON. Amaethon was said to have stolen from ARAWN, the lord of the otherworld ANNWN, a hound, a deer and a bird, and as a result caused the Cad Goddeu or Battle of Trees. It was in this battle that Amaethon's brother, GWYDION,

magically transformed trees into warriors to fight in the battle.

AMAIRGEN, sometimes known as Amergin, was one of the first Irish druids, the ancient priests in Celtic lands. He came to Ireland with the Milesians. These children of MILESIUS, or Mil, who was a leader of the Celts who lived in Spain, were believed to be the ancestors of the present-day Irish. Having defeated the divine rulers of Ireland, the TUATHA DE DANANN, the Milesians could not agree on which of their leaders should be king. Two sons of Mil, Eremon and EBER, contested the throne and for the sake of peace the island was divided into two kingdoms, one in the north, the other in the south. However, peace was not to survive for long, and renewed fighting between the followers of the two

AMAIRGEN (above) was one of the first druids in Ireland. He possessed both spiritual and political authority, and pronounced the first judgement in the land, deciding who would be the first king. An inspired shaman and seer, he is credited with a mystical poem in the Book of Invasions. (ILLUSTRATION ANON.)

brothers plunged the country once again into dreadful strife. The fighting came to an end only with the death of Eber. Amairgen then installed Eremon as High King of Ireland at Tara. Even then conflicts still occurred because of the ceaseless rivalries between lesser rulers.

AMFORTAS see PELLES.

ANNWN was a Welsh otherworld that was an idyllic land of peace and plenty. In Annwn there was a fountain of sweet wine and a cauldron of rebirth, which, it would seem, was the basis of the medieval Grail myth. In one Welsh tradition, ARTHUR lost most of his warriors in a disastrous attempt to seize this magic cauldron.

The lord of Annwn was the grey-clad ARAWN, with whom the Dyfed chieftain PWYLL agreed to exchange shapes and responsibilities for a year. Arawn had a pack of hounds, the Celtic "hounds of hell", which were believed to fly at night in pursuit of human souls. (See also CELTIC OTHERWORLDS; WONDROUS CAULDRONS)

ANNWN (below), a Welsh otherworld, was a land of fruitfulness and rest, filled with the song of birds. Annwn's magical cauldron, guarded by nine maidens, healed the sick and restored the dead to life. A recurrent motif in Celtic myth, magic cauldrons feature in the tales of Bran and Dagda. (ILLUSTRATION BY NICK BEALE, 1995.)

ANU, a great earth goddess and mother of all the heroes, was known as the "lasting one" and also as Dana, mother of the Tuatha De Danann. In Munster there are two hills known as the Paps of Anu because they symbolized her breasts. (ILLUSTRATION BY GLENN STEWARD, 1995.)

ANU, sometimes called Danu or Dana, was the mother goddess of Irish mythology. The TUATHA DE DANANN ("the people of the goddess Dana") were her divine children and the gods and goddesses who ruled Ireland prior to the arrival of the Milesians. It is quite possible that the monks who wrote down the Irish sagas from the fifth century onwards underplayed the original role of goddesses in their compilations. Certainly, the stories they recorded show us a man's world, a place where warriors seem most at home. The cult of Anu was especially associated with Munster, and two hills in County Kerry are still known as Da Chich Anann ("The Paps of Anu").

AOIFA, sometimes known as Aoife, was the daughter of Ard-Greimne and an Irish warrior-princess in the Land of Shadows, an otherworld kingdom. Her sister SCATHACH instructed the Ulster hero CUCHULAINN in the arts of war. But when the sisters went to war Scathach was frightened to take the hero with her into battle in case Aoifa killed him. Undeterred by Aoifa's reputation as a fighter, Cuchulainn challenged her to single combat. Before the fight took place, Cuchulainn asked Scathach what Aoifa loved best and Scathach told him that above all else she treasured her chariot. At first the combat went as expected in Aoifa's favour, but Cuchulainn distracted her attention at a critical moment by calling out that her chariot horse was in trouble. Afterwards, Aoifa became Cuchulainn's lover and bore him a son named CONLAI. It was, however, the boy's fate to be killed by his own father.

AONGHUS was the Irish love god. His father was DAGDA, the father of the gods and the protector of druids, and his mother was the water goddess BOANN. Rather like Zeus, Dagda deceived Boann's husband and lay with her. The monks who wrote down the Irish sagas tried to legitimize the birth by making Boann the wife of Dagda, but it is obvious that Aonghus was a divine love-child.

Aonghus was handsome and four birds always hovered above his head which were said to represent kisses. Birds also feature in his courtship of CAER, a girl of divine descent who came from Connacht and lived as a swan. Her father, Ethal, was one of the TUATHA DE DANANN. He seems to have been reluctant about the marriage until Aonghus' father, Dagda, made Ethal his prisoner. It was finally agreed that Aonghus could marry Caer provided he could identify her and she was willing to be his bride. On the feast of Samhain, Aonghus found Caer swimming on a lake with a hundred and fifty other swans. He instantly recognized her and she agreed to marry him.

An interesting tale that has attached itself to Aonghus concerns his foster-son DIARMUID UA DUIBHNE, or "Diarmuid of the Love Spot". This attractive young man received a magic love spot on his forehead from a mysterious girl one

ARAWN, king of Annwn, strides through his enchanted forest accompanied by his flying hounds, the Celtic "hounds of hell", one of whose duties was to escort souls on their journey to the otherworld. Like some other fairy creatures, they appear white with red ears, a token of the otherworld. (ILLUSTRATION BY JAMES ALEXANDER, 1995.)

night during a hunt. From then on, no woman could ever see Diarmuid without loving him. This included GRAINNE, the princess who had been promised by the High King of Ireland to his Fenian commander FINN MACCOOL. Aonghus saved the lovers from the great warrior's wrath, but he could not protect Diarmuid from the fate given to him at birth by the gods, that he should be killed by a magic boar. Nevertheless, Aonghus brought Diarmuid's body back to his own palace at New Grange, on the banks of the River Boyne, where he breathed a new soul into it so that he could talk to his foster-son.

ARAWN was the ruler of the Welsh otherworld ANNWN, which was a paradise of peace and plenty. The Dyfed chieftain PWYLL became friends with Arawn and was allowed to claim in his title some authority over the otherworld. The two rulers met by chance. While out hunting, Pwyll encountered a strange pack of hounds chasing a stag, so he drove them off and set

AOIFA, a warrior-princess from the Land of Shadows, spars with her young son, Conlai, instructing him in the martial arts. The tradition of warrior-women was strong in Celtic society, where women bore arms as late as AD 700, and where the fiercest gods were often women. (ILLUSTRATION BY JAMES ALEXANDER, 1995.)

AONGHUS (left), an engaging god of love and courtesy, a Celtic equivalent of Eros, appears in this fanciful portrayal as a charming, if somewhat whimsical character, who calms the foamy sea with his fairy magic. (AONGHUS, GOD OF LOVE AND COURTESY, PUTTING A SPELL OF SUMMER CALM ON THE SEA BY JOHN DUNCAN, CANVAS, DETAIL, 1908.)

ART (above) confronts an army of savage and venomous giant toads on his perilous journey through the Land of Wonder, in search of Delbchaem. A taboo laid on the young hero by the jealous goddess Becuma, forced him to find and win the lovely girl imprisoned by her wicked parents. (ILLUSTRATION BY ARTHUR RACKHAM, C. 1900.)

than she gave birth to DYLAN and LLEU. GWYDION, Arianrhod's brother, immediately took charge of Lleu and brought him up, but this did not prevent Arianrhod placing a series of taboos upon him, including the stricture that he was to have no wife in the human race.

ART, in Irish mythology, was the son of Conn of the Hundred Battles. In one myth, Conn's jealous mistress, the goddess Becuma Cneisgel, contrived to send Art off on a perilous journey through the Land of Wonder in search of Delbchaem ("Fair Shape"). After facing untold dangers, he managed to find and rescue Delbchaem. Art's son by another woman was CORMAC MAC ART. Art was killed by the rebel Lugaide Mac Con in the battle of Moy Muchruinne.

his own hounds on to the prey. Just as the stag was about to fall, a grey-clad figure appeared and rebuked Pwyll for this discourtesy in the field. It was Arawn. In order to placate Arawn and to gain his friendship, Pwyll accepted a proposal that he should exchange forms with him for a year and then slay Arawn's enemy, Havgan. It was also agreed that Pwyll would share the bed of Arawn's queen for the

same period of time, but without making love to her.

Arawn warned Pwyll that he must kill Havgan by a single blow, for if struck a second time he instantly revived. When Pwyll and Havgan fought, the Welsh chieftain dealt him a fatal blow and ignored Havgan's plea to finish him off with another strike. As a result of this service, Arawn and Pwyll became close allies and Dyfed prospered.

ARIANRHOD was the daughter of the Welsh goddess DON and niece of MATH, king of Gwynedd. Math could sleep only if his feet were held in a virgin's lap, and when Goewin, the virgin who usually acted this part for him was raped by his nephew Gilvaethwy, it was suggested that Arianrhod should take her place. To test her purity Arianrhod had to step over Math's wand. No sooner had she done so

ARTHUR is undoubtedly the best known of the Celtic heroes. He was most popular during the Middle Ages, when the exploits of his followers, the Knights of the Round Table, impressed the greater part of western Europe. It was with some misgivings that the Church permitted a Christianized version of these Celtic myths to occupy such an important place in the medieval imagination. It was never quite at ease with the story of the Grail, or *SANGREAL*, which *JOSEPH OF ARIMATHEA* was believed to have brought to Britain, since its miraculous properties were clearly derived from the Celtic cauldron, a vessel of plenty as well as of rebirth. The strength of popular feeling for the Arthurian myth can be appreciated by a riot that occurred in 1113 at the town of Bodmin in Cornwall because the French servants of visiting nobility denied Arthur's undeath.

Although some of the earliest stories concerning Arthur are found in Welsh poems of the seventh century, there can be little doubt that the warlike king belongs to the heroic traditions of both Ireland and Wales. He appears in several

ARTHUR, a child of destiny, was guarded and guided by spiritual forces from birth. Smuggled out of Tintagel Castle by Merlin, the mage, he was fostered in safety and secrecy, unaware of his destiny until his rightful time to draw the sword from the stone, thus proving his birthright. (MERLIN AND ARTHUR BY W HATHERELL, CANVAS, C. 1910.)

Irish sagas, one of which describes how he stole the hounds of the Fenian leader *FINN MACCOOL* on one of his daring raids. Indeed, as a warrior, hunter of magic boars, killer of giants, witches and monsters, and as leader of a band of heroes whose adventures led them into untold mysteries and marvels, Arthur had much in common with Finn MacCool. But according to the ninth-century monk Nennius, Arthur was a historical leader who rallied the people of Britain against Anglo-Saxon invaders after the Roman legions had gone. Nennius credits Arthur with twelve victories, but does not mention the account of his death recorded slightly later in a history of Wales, which states that Arthur and his sworn enemy *MODRED* both fell in 537 at the battle of Camluan.

Arthur was the son of the British king *UTHER PENDRAGON* and Igraine, wife of the Cornish duke Gorlois. He was conceived out of wedlock and brought up away from his parents by the wizard *MERLIN*. The resourceful Merlin had already designed for Uther Pendragon a wonderful stronghold and placed in it the famous Round Table, at which one hundred and fifty knights could be seated. This unusual piece of furniture may

ARTHUR, prompted by Merlin, asks the Lady of the Lake for the sword, Excalibur. The young king marvelled at the shining sword but Merlin insisted that the scabbard was worth ten of the swords because it prevented loss of blood in battle. (ILLUSTRATION BY AUBREY BEARDSLEY, C. 1870.)

have a connection with Joseph of Arimathea, not least because it had a special place reserved for the Grail. While Joseph of Arimathea was imprisoned in Palestine, the Grail is said to have kept him alive. Later he brought it to Britain, where it disappeared due to people's sinfulness. Thus the recovery of the Grail became the great quest of Arthur's knights.

When Uther Pendragon died, the Knights of the Round Table were at a loss to know who should be the next king. They decided that Merlin should guide them. The wizard told them that they would know who Uther's successor was when he drew a magic sword from a stone, which had mysteriously appeared in London. Many knights tried to pull the sword from the stone, but none could move it.

After a number of years Arthur journeyed to London to watch his first tournament. A knight who had been appointed by Merlin to act as the boy's guardian was taking part, but finding he was without a sword, he sent Arthur to get one. Without realizing the significance of the sword in the stone, Arthur pulled it out and gave it to the amazed knight. Thus was the heir of Uther Pendragon revealed.

Even then, there were knights who would not accept Arthur as

ARTHUR, at rest in an enchanted forest, gazes in wonder at the amazing Questing Beast at the well. It was a ferlie or bewitching otherworldly wonder, which defied capture. Sir Pellinore and later Sir Palomides spent years in futile pursuit of the tantalizing chimaera. (ILLUSTRATION BY AUBREY BEARDSLEY, C. 1870.)

ARTHUR'S Round Table served many purposes: it prevented quarrels over precedence; symbolized wholeness; and commemorated the Table of the Last Supper, with the Grail at the centre. (KING ARTHUR AND THE KNIGHTS OF THE ROUND TABLE SUMMONED TO THE QUEST BY A STRANGE DAMSEL BY E BURNE-JONES, TAPESTRY, 1898–99.)

king. Only with Merlin's aid was the young ruler able to defeat his opponents and bring peace to Britain. How much he depended on magic became obvious to Arthur early in his reign. Having drawn his own sword without cause against one of his knights, Arthur was dismayed to see the blade shatter. Merlin saved him by putting the knight to sleep, for Arthur was otherwise unarmed. In despair the king wandered along the shore of a lake when, to his amazement, he saw a hand and arm rise out of the water, holding another magic sword. This was the famous Excalibur, his sure support, according to the Lady of the Lake, who handed it to him.

Rearmed and reassured, Arthur went on to be a great king. He defeated the Anglo-Saxons, aided King Leodegraunce of Scotland in his wars against the Irish and even campaigned as far away from his kingdom as Rome. In return for the aid given to Leodegraunce, Arthur was betrothed to his daughter GUINEVERE. At first Merlin objected to the match, since he knew of Guinevere's love for Sir *LANCELOT*, the most handsome of the Knights of the Round Table. But he later blessed the married couple and, according to one version of the myth, gave Arthur the Round Table as a wedding gift. Nevertheless, the queen and Lancelot were soon lovers, and when Arthur found out about his wife's unfaithfulness Lancelot fled to Brittany.

Arthur pursued Sir Lancelot and besieged him in his Breton stronghold. The siege had to be lifted, however, because news reached the king that his nephew Sir Modred had seized Camelot and even forced Guinevere to consent to marriage, after spreading stories of the king's death on campaign. Returning to Britain, Arthur summoned his knights to do battle with the rebels. Prior to the conflict, it was agreed that the king and his nephew would meet between the two armies to discuss the possibility of peace. Because neither one trusted the other, each ordered his forces to attack if they saw anyone draw a sword. When a knight unsheathed his weapon to kill a snake, a terrible battle was fought, in which the flower of British chivalry fell.

Only two of Arthur's knights were left alive on a battlefield that was covered by the dead and dying. Although he had won, King Arthur had to be carried away by these knights, such was the severity of his wound. Knowing his own end was near, he had Excalibur thrown into a lake, where a hand swiftly seized it. Then Arthur boarded a magic boat and disappeared. His last words were that he was going to *AVALON* to be cured of his wounds so that he might return one day to lead his people once more.

The inscription on Arthur's tomb at Glastonbury picks up this Celtic idea of reincarnation. It reads: "Here lies Arthur, king that was, king that shall be." Such an undeath was not enough to save his weakened kingdom from the Anglo-Saxons, however. The whole of the Arthurian myth turns on the disintegration of the chivalric unity that was established by the Round Table, but which was finally destroyed by the implacable hatred between Arthur and Modred. (See also *MAGIC AND ENCHANTMENT; HEROIC QUESTS*)

ARTHUR rests in peace in Avalon, guarded by four fairy queens. Morgan le Fay, cowled in black, consults her book of magic crafts, to heal the wounds of the "undead" king. The winged apparition carrying the Grail symbolizes the hope and future promise of Arthur's reign. (LA MORT D'ARTHUR BY JAMES ARCHER, CANVAS, 1860.)

B

AVALON was another name for the Welsh otherworld, *ANNWN*, and its name suggests that it was an island of apples. The mortally wounded *ARTHUR* was ferried there by three mysterious women in a black boat, following the terrible battle against Sir *MODRED*'s army. The undead king was expected to return from Avalon and lead the oppressed Celtic population of Britain to victory over their Anglo-Saxon and, later, Norman conquerors. According to one version of the myth, Excalibur was forged there. Traditionally, Avalon has been identified with Glastonbury, the supposed site of Arthur's tomb. (See also *CELTIC OTHERWORLDS*)

BADB (meaning "crow") was an Irish goddess of battle. She was one of a group of war deities who could influence the outcome of conflict by inspiring the combatants with fear or courage. The others were known as *MORRIGAN*, *NEMAIN* and *MACHA*. Myth connects Badb with the historical battle of Clontarf in 1014, when the High King Brian defeated the Viking invaders and Badb was said to have appeared over the warriors' heads.

BALOR, a formidable one-eyed god of death, led the misshapen Fomorii against the younger Tuatha De Danann. Here his grandson, Lugh, casts a fatal stone into Balor's deadly eye, forcing it back through his head where its lethal gaze destroys his warriors marching behind him.
(ILLUSTRATION BY MIRANDA GRAY, 1995.)

BALOR was the Irish Cyclops. This one-eyed god of death was the most formidable of the *FOMORII*, the violent and monstrous sea gods who ruled Ireland before the arrival of the *TUATHA DE DANANN*. So dreadful was his one eye that he destroyed whoever he looked upon and his eyelid had to be levered up by four servants. It was prophesied that he would be slain by his own grandson. To avoid this fate he locked his only daughter *ETHLINN* in a crystal tower on Tory Island, off the north-west coast of Ireland. Even so, Balor was killed in battle with a sling-shot by the sun god *LUGH*, Ethlinn's son and the champion of the Tuatha De Danann.

Lugh's father was Cian, a lesser member of the Tuatha De Danann. With the assistance of a female druid, Cian had entered the crystal tower and slept with Ethlinn. When Balor learned that his daughter had given birth to three sons, he ordered that they be drowned in a whirlpool near Tory Island. Balor's servants duly rolled them up in a sheet, but on the way to the whirlpool one of the boys fell out unnoticed. Either the druid then handed the fortunate baby to the smith god *GOIBHNIU*, or alternatively *MANANNAN MAC LIR*, the god of the sea, decided to foster him. In either event, Lugh was saved and set on the road to his destiny as the slayer of Balor.

The fateful meeting between Lugh and Balor occurred at the second battle of Magh Tuireadh, a fierce contest between the Fomorii and the Tuatha De Danann. Nobody could stand Balor's lethal gaze, not even the Tuatha De Danann leader *NUADA*, the owner of a sword which previously none could escape. The battle was just turning into a Tuatha De Danann rout, when Lugh noticed that the

BANSHEE, or bean sidhe, women of the fairies, lived underground in sparkling sidhe – fairy heavens hidden beneath grassy mounds on Irish hillsides. Legend has it that a banshee attaches itself to a family and warns of impending death with an eerie wail. (ILLUSTRATION BY H J FORD, 1902.)

AVALON, Arthur's last resting place, was an otherworldly retreat of wonder, mystery and peace. Its nine guardian queens recall an actual, historical order of nine nuns who lived off the coast of Roman Brittany, as well as the nine mythical maidens guarding Annwn's magic cauldron. (KING ARTHUR IN AVALON BY E BURNE-JONES, CANVAS, 1894.)

single eyelid of Balor was slowly closing through weariness. Lugh crept near to him with a magic sling-shot in hand. The moment the eyelid opened again, he hurled the stone so hard that it forced the eyeball backward through Balor's head, with the result that it was the Fomorii who now suffered from the destructive effect of its paralysing stare. The Tuatha De Danann were able to defeat the Fomorii, who were driven from Ireland for ever. (See also *CELTIC OTHERWORLDS*)

BANSHEE is the modern name for the *bean sidhe* ("woman of the fairies"), the traditional fairy of the Irish countryside. After the arrival of the Milesians from what is now Spain (the ancestors of the present-day Irish) the gods and goddesses known as the *TUATHA DE DANANN* disappeared underground and dwelt in mounds, and over the centuries they were slowly transformed in the popular imagination into fairies. It was believed that the wailing of a banshee foretold the approach of a human death.

BEDIVERE see BEDWYR

BEDWYR, according to Welsh mythology, was a one-handed warrior who, together with his friend and companion *KAI*, played an important part in helping *CULHWCH* to procure the prizes he required to win the hand of *OLWEN*. They were both members of King *ARTHUR*'s court. In later Arthurian romance Bedwyr became Sir Bedivere, the faithful knight who remained with King Arthur after he was mortally wounded, threw the sword Excalibur into the lake on the king's instructions and bore his body to the boat which carried him to *AVALON*.

BEL see BELENUS

BELENUS, also known as Bel, was a Celtic sun god known to the Romans. Julius Caesar compared Belenus to Apollo, the god of prophecy. He appears in various forms across the Celtic world, as Beli to the Welsh, Bile to the Irish and Belenus to the Gauls. Beltaine,

one of the important festivals of the Celtic calendar, was celebrated on the first of May in his honour, and his name survives in a number of place names such as Billingsgate, "Bile's gate" (formerly a fish market in London). Although his worship was clearly widespread, little else is known about him.

BEN DIGEIDFRAN see BRAN THE BLESSED

BILE see BELENUS

BLATHNAT was the wife of King *CU ROI* of Munster. She fell in love with *CUCHULAINN*, the great Ulster hero and enemy of Cu Roi, and betrayed her husband's people by showing the hero how he could enter her husband's apparently impregnable fortress. A stream flowed through the fort and when Blathnat poured milk into the

BELENUS, a Celtic sun god, was honoured on the eve of Beltaine when Celts lit bonfires, the "fires of Bel", symbolizing the rays of the sun and the promise of summer fruitfulness. Here, the fairies, once Celtic gods, ride out from their hollow hills to celebrate Beltaine. (THE RIDERS OF THE SIDHE BY JOHN DUNCAN, CANVAS, 1911.)

water, Cuchulainn was able to follow its course. In the fierce battle that followed Cu Roi was killed and Cuchulainn was able to ride off with Blathnat. He also took with him Cu Roi's bard, Fer Cherdne. When the party halted on a cliff top, however, Fer Cherdne took the opportunity to avenge his former master's death by grabbing hold of Blathnat and jumping over the edge with her in his arms.

BEDWYR guarded Arthur at the end of his life, as they waited by a lake for the ship that would ferry the king to Avalon. This evocative scene blends photographic realism with a ghostly backdrop to create an effective and convincing representation of an otherworldly realm. (MORT D'ARTHUR BY JOHN GARRICK, CANVAS, 1862.)

CELTIC OTHERWORLDS

T HE GLITTERING OTHERWORLDS of Celtic myth are the invisible realms of gods and spirits, fairies, elves and misshapen giants. Some are sparkling heavens and some are brooding hells. The veil between the visible and invisible worlds is gossamer-thin and easily torn. Seers and bards pass in and out on spirit-flights or journeys of the soul, as do some privileged heroes, such as all-knowing Finn MacCool, or the intrepid voyagers, Bran, Brendan and Maeldun. Some heroes, such as Cuchulainn, pay only fleeting visits; while Oisin returned from his otherworldly trip 300 years after his time. Common gateways to the otherworld are by water and across narrow bridges, beneath mounds or wells which hide sparkling underground heavens, or dark purgatories. On the eve of Samhain, October 31, all the gates to the otherworld open and wondrous spirits emerge from under the hollow hills.

THOMAS THE RHYMER (above right), like all inspired bards, slipped in and out of the otherworld, drawing on divine sources of inspiration for his poetry. Bards, like druids, possessed supernatural powers of prophecy and inspiration when seized by Awen, the divine muse. Their power to satirize with the glam dicin, an undermining song, made them more feared than fierce warriors. Here, the poet is visited by a being from the otherworld, possibly his divine muse. (THOMAS THE RHYMER AND THE QUEEN OF FAERIE BY J N PATON, CANVAS, C. 1890.)

CELTIC FAIRIES (right) ride out from their underground palaces on the eve of Beltaine to celebrate Belenus' feast. The splendid riders bear treasures from the otherworld; on the left, a wand of intelligence and Tree of Knowledge, and on the right, the recurrent Cauldron of Plenty. The solemn mood and glittering Celtic jewellery and harness create a convincing and haunting portrayal of lordly beings from another world. (THE RIDERS OF THE SIDHE BY JOHN DUNCAN, CANVAS, DETAIL, 1911.)

CARBONEK (above), the Grail Castle of Arthurian legend, was an otherworldly heaven guarded by angels and wondrous spirits whose unearthly song was beautiful beyond imagining. The castle housed the Grail, a holy vessel, said to be the Cup of the Last Supper, which contained healing spiritual sustenance. Lancelot was ferried to Carbonek on a ghostly ship without captain or crew and permitted a distant vision of the sacred chalice because of his courageous spirit. His love of Guinevere forbade a complete vision. (ILLUSTRATION BY ALAN LEE, 1984.)

BALOR (above) and his misshapen people, the Fomorii, symbolize the dark forces of the otherworld. Before their defeat at the hands of the Tuatha De Danann, they oppressed the Irish with crushing tributes and cruelty. While the Tuatha De Danann lived underground in glittering sidhe, the Fomorii roamed beneath lakes and seas in bleak purgatories. Balor's single eye, poisoned in youth, paralysed his enemies with its deadly gaze. (ILLUSTRATION BY ALAN LEE, 1984.)

PWYLL, riding through a lush, wooded idyll, suddenly found himself in the otherworldly realm of Annwn. After driving off some shining white hounds from a fallen stag, he encountered Arawn, the grey-clad lord of Annwn. Like the Greek god of the underworld Hades, Arawn may possibly symbolize a Lord of Winter, because he fought an annual battle with Havgan ("Summer Song"). On one occasion, he asked Pwyll to swap places with him for a year, at the end of which Pwyll fought and won the seasonal duel. (ILLUSTRATION BY ALAN LEE, 1984.)

BLODEUEDD (whose name means "born of flowers" or "flower face") was a beautiful, magical woman. She was conjured by *MATH* and *GWYDION* from the blossoms of oak, broom and meadowsweet to be the wife of *LLEU*, Gwydion's nephew, because Lleu's mother, *ARIANRHOD*, had declared that he should marry no mortal woman. For a time the young couple lived together happily, but one day Lleu went to visit Math and while he was away Blodeuedd kindly offered hospitality to a passing huntsman, Goronwy, the lord of Penllyn. Blodeuedd and Goronwy fell in love and began to plot the murder of Lleu. This was no easy task, for Lleu could be killed only while standing with one foot on a goat's back and the other on the edge of a bath tub, and only by a spear which it had taken a full year to make. However, even though the pair finally succeeded in meeting all the conditions and attacked him, he did not die but flew into the air in the shape of an eagle. Math and Gwydion set out to avenge Lleu. When they found Blodeuedd, Gwydion turned her into an owl, the bird of the night.

BOANN was a water goddess and the mother of *AONGHUS*, the Irish god of love. According to the different versions of her myth, she was married either to *NECHTAN* or to Elcmar. *DAGDA*, the chief god of the *TUATHA DE DANANN*, was her lover and the father of Aonghus. He was able to seduce Boann by sending her husband on a nine-month journey that seemed but one day.

BRAN, son of Febal, is the hero of the most famous of the Irish voyage myths. Sea voyages fascinated the Irish storytellers, who would tell of strange adventures on remote islands, including those of otherworlds, such as the home of gods and goddesses, as well as the place where souls briefly rested before rebirth. Bran's great journey began

BLODEUEDD (above), the fairest woman in the world, was conjured out of blossoms by the magicians Gwydion and Math, so that she could be the wife of Gwydion's nephew, Lleu. But she betrayed her husband for another man. Gwydion, here, watches as his beautiful creation comes to life. (ILLUSTRATION BY ALAN LEE, 1984.)

BOANN (below), a water goddess and the mother of Aonghus, violated the sanctity of a sacred well of inspiration. In outrage the waters bubbled and swelled, forming a torrent which became the River Boyne, which is named after her. In its current swam the Salmon of Knowledge, seen here. (ILLUSTRATION BY ARTHUR RACKHAM, C.1910.)

when he found a silver branch that was covered with white flowers. Gathering his kinsmen together, Bran displayed the magic bough, only to be surprised by the sudden appearance of a woman dressed in very unusual cloth. She sang to the assembled company of the great wonders to be found in the lands beyond the sea, the otherworld islands, each larger than Ireland, and inhabited by beautiful women who had no knowledge of sorrow, sickness or death. Happiness, she sang to them, was the lot of all living in these wonderful lands. Then the strange woman stopped singing and vanished, taking the magic bough with her. Bran had been unable to hold on to it, even with both his hands.

The next day Bran sailed westwards with twenty-seven kinsmen. Their first encounter was with the sea god *MANANNAN MAC LIR*, who was driving his chariot across the waves. Once again the Irish heroes were informed by the sea god of the marvels that awaited them. Even then the sea appeared to be a plain of flowers, with blossoming shrubs and an orchard of fruitful trees. That day Bran's boat came to the Isle of Merriment, where his crew could hardly stand up for laughing, and then in the evening they reached the Isle of Women. The beautiful women's leader called to Bran to step ashore, but he was afraid to land; so she threw a ball of thread that stuck to Bran's hand, and by magic drew the boat from the waves. When they came ashore the Irish heroes found soft beds and delicious food ready for them. The delightful stay seemed to them to last for only a year, but in fact many years had passed. When one of the crew grew homesick and persuaded Bran that it was time that they sailed home, he was warned by the chief woman not to set foot on soil again. Arriving off the Irish coast, Bran discovered that nobody recognized him, and he was known only as a legendary figure who had long ago embarked on a great voyage to the otherworlds, so he set sail again; but not before one desperate hero forgot the warning and jumped ashore, and immediately turned into a pile of ash, as though he had been dead for centuries.

The voyage of Bran is certainly an ancient myth, although it was not written down until the eighth century by monks. Even though the monks added certain Christian elements such as references to Jesus Christ and Adam's sin, they did not obscure the tale's original magical atmosphere. (See also *FABULOUS VOYAGES*)

BRAN (below), on his epic voyage, visited the Isle of Women, where the chief woman brought his ship to shore with magic thread. Here, she holds a cup of plenty, symbolizing the idyllic delights of the island. The voyagers stayed for what they thought was a year before they left for home.
(ILLUSTRATION BY DANUTA MEYER, 1993.)

BRAN THE BLESSED, the son of the sea god Llyr, played a different role to *BRAN*, son of Febal. In Welsh mythology, he was called Bendigeidfran and seems to have been an otherworld god, although he was also active as a British king in mortal affairs. He allowed his sister *BRANWEN* to marry the Irish king *MATHOLWCH*, without the consent of her half-brother *EFNISIEN*.

Because of this slight, Efnisien cut off the lips, ears and tails of Matholwch's horses during the wedding feast in Wales. Not unnaturally, hostilities almost broke out between the Irish and the Britons as a result, but Bran

BRAN THE BLESSED (right), the mighty ruler of Britain, sailed to Ireland to rescue his beautiful sister, Branwen. In the ensuing battle, Bran was mortally wounded, but his head, cut from his body, lived on. His magical cauldron of rebirth is seen here, restored, along with his head.
(ILLUSTRATION BY ALAN LEE, 1984.)

managed to avoid a war by presenting Matholwch with a magic cauldron. This otherworld vessel could bring men back to life, but without restoring their speech.

Back in Ireland, Matholwch was unable to convince his warriors that Bran's gift was adequate compensation for the damage done to the horses. So Branwen ceased to be the Irish queen and was made to work in the palace kitchens, even though she had already given Matholwch a son and heir, *GWERN*. When Bran learned of how she was being treated, he raised a great army and sailed to Ireland. In the ensuing battle the Britons slew every Irish man there was, but only

seven of their own army survived. Even Bran was killed, by a wound caused by a poisoned arrow. On his deathbed he told his followers to cut off his head, which apparently was still able to eat and talk during the voyage home. A later addition to the myth says that the head was brought to London and buried facing Europe, to ward off foreign invaders. King Arthur is said to have used the head for its power.

The Celts believed that heads were the seat of the soul, which may partly explain their practice of head-hunting. Even more curious, was the medieval Christian claim that Bran was the first British man. (See also *WONDROUS CAULDRONS*)

BRANGAINE (above) and Iseult peer quizzically at the shy young stranger in the palace garden, puzzling over his identity. But as soon as the dog leapt fondly onto his lap, they recognized the stranger as Tristan, who had been assumed dead. They were confused at first because he was much changed after his wanderings in the wildwood. (ILLUSTRATION BY EVELYN PAUL, C. 1920.)

BRANGAINE was the maid of *ISEULT*, princess of Ireland and lover of *TRISTAN*. Iseult had been promised in marriage to King *MARK* of Cornwall. Tristan, his nephew, came to Ireland to escort her across the sea. Before the ship sailed, Iseult's mother gave Brangaine a love potion for Iseult and Mark on their wedding night, as it caused those who drank it to love only each other for the rest of their lives. However, during the voyage, Tristan became thirsty and unwittingly drank the potion, and then offered some to Iseult.

Through all the ensuing difficulties Brangaine was always loyal, sharing their secrets, such as when Tristan was brought to Mark's castle mistaken for a wild man, even taking Iseult's place in Mark's bed on the wedding night.

BRANWEN (right) releases a starling, bearing a plea for help, across the sea to her giant brother, Bran. When he reads of her plight in Ireland, he sets sail immediately with a Welsh fleet. (ILLUSTRATION BY ALAN LEE, 1984.)

BRANWEN was the daughter of Llyr, the Welsh equivalent of the Irish sea god LIR, and sister to BRAN THE BLESSED, and MANAWYDAN. When High King MATHOLWCH of Ireland came to Bran's court at Harlech it was agreed that Branwen should be given to him in marriage. But her half-brother EFNISIEN was not consulted and, feeling insulted, he cut off the lips, ears and tails of Matholwch's horses. To restore peace Bran offered the Irish king replacement horses and a magic cauldron. Matholwch returned to Ireland with Branwen, who was at first received with great rejoicing for she was generous with gifts, and before long she gave birth to a son, GWERN. But after a few years Matholwch's friends and family began to complain that the compensation he had received from Bran was not enough. To satisfy them, Matholwch insisted that Branwen relinquish her position as queen and become a cook for the court.

During the next three years, as Branwen worked in the palace kitchens, she reared a starling and taught it to recognize her brother Bran. Then she sent it across the sea with a letter tied to its leg, telling of her treatment. When Bran and the Britons learned of her fate they brought an army to Ireland.

BRENDAN the Navigator was the title given to a sixth-century Irish saint. Indeed, the account of the two voyages undertaken by St Brendan was just as popular in the Middle Ages as the stories told about the Knights of the Round Table. This wonder tale is in the same tradition as that of BRAN, son of Febal, although its direct inspiration was the voyage of the Aran hero MAELDUN. Having taken holy orders, Brendan prayed to go on a pilgrimage into unknown lands. An angel then showed him an island in a vision. In search of this beautiful land, St Brendan set sail twice, first in a craft made from skins, and

BRENDAN, the Irish saint and navigator, returns to Ireland after his wondrous voyage in search of the Land of Promise. His tour of twelve mysterious islands included a land of birdlike spirits, which was possibly the Land of Promise. His amazing tale seems to be a blend of earlier voyages. (ILLUSTRATION BY JAMES STEPHENS, C. 1920.)

second in a boat made of wood. Miraculous events took place due to the saint's faith. One Easter a whale appeared so that St Brendan and his followers could hold a service on its broad back. After the service, the whale plunged under the waves and swam away. This great animal was made docile by St Brendan, as were numerous whirlpools. Even the Devil was unable to disturb the saint's serenity when he showed him the pain of Hell. St Brendan also restored to life one of the monks who were his companions after he had insisted on seeing this forbidden sight for himself.

On the voyages he also encountered a heathen giant, whom he baptized, terrifying mice and an enormous sea cat. Finally, they reached the island in St Brendan's vision. Inhabited by a hermit clothed in feathers, it was probably the Land of Promise, a place of Christian resurrection similar to the Celtic otherworlds. On his return to Ireland, St Brendan refused to stay in his old monastery but moved instead to a retreat near Limerick, where he died. (See also *FABULOUS VOYAGES*)

BRES, in Irish mythology, was briefly the leader of the *TUATHA DE DANANN*, the implacable enemies of the *FOMORII*, the sea gods who ruled Ireland long before them. Bres was an unusual leader of the Tuatha De Danann because his father was *ELATHA*, who was a Fomorii king of a land that lay under the sea. Elatha had met a Tuatha De Danann goddess named Eri on the sea-shore and made love to her on the sand. Bres was born as a result, although Eri was careful to say nothing to her husband about the boy's real father.

When Bres grew up, he fought against the existing inhabitants of Ireland, the *FIRBOLG*, at the first battle of Magh Tuireadh. In this engagement *NUADA*, the leader of the invading Tuatha De Danann, lost a hand and in consequence he retired for a time. Nuada tried to use a silver replacement without success, until Miach, son of the healing god *DIAN CECHT*, made him a hand of flesh and blood. However, until Nuada was fully recovered and able to resume his

BRIAN and his brothers set out on a perilous voyage across the world to fulfil eight tasks, set by the sun god Lugh. With daring and resource they sought and found wondrous treasures, such as an invincible sword and healing pigskin, which helped the De Danann in their battle with the Fomorii. (ILLUSTRATION BY STEPHEN REID, 1912.)

leadership, the De Danann were under the command of Bres. But Bres had no gift for leadership and became something of a tyrant. On the restoration of Nuada, Bres and his mother Eri fled to Elatha in order to seek Fomorii assistance. This caused the second battle of Magh Tuireadh, in which Nuada was killed. Through the bravery of the sun god *LUGH*, however, the Fomorii were routed and Bres was taken prisoner. One version of the myth explains how, in return for his life, Bres promised to instruct the Tuatha De Danann in the arts of planting and sowing crops. It is possible that Bres, like his wife, the fertility goddess *BRIGID*, was a deity connected with agriculture.

BRIAN was one of the three sons of *TUIREANN*, whose family were engaged in a feud with the family of Cian, father of the god *LUGH*. When Lugh sent Cian to summon the warriors of the *TUATHA DE DANANN* to battle, Brian and his brothers, Iuchar and Iucharba, killed him during his journey. To atone for this act of murder they were given by Lugh eight tasks to perform. Among the objects they had to retrieve were three apples from the Gardens of the Sun, a healing pigskin from the king of Greece, a poisoned spear from the king of Persia, a cooking-spit belonging to the nymphs of an undersea kingdom and the seven pigs of King Asal of the Golden Pillars, which could be cooked and eaten one day and found alive the next. Finally, they were to shout three times on the Hill of Mochaen. Having successfully brought back to Lugh all the magical objects he required, they then set out to perform their last duty. However, they were mortally wounded by Mochaen and his sons. Tuireann therefore asked Lugh if he might borrow the magical pigskin and so heal his sons, but the god refused and Brian and his brothers died. (See also *FABULOUS VOYAGES*)

B

ST BRIDE *is ferried by angels from Iona to Bethlehem on the eve of Christ's birth to foster the infant Christ. Celtic and Christian motifs merge in this scene, while the angels' soaring flight beyond the frame enhances the powerfully spiritual effect.*

(ST BRIDE BY JOHN DUNCAN, CANVAS, C. 1913.)

BRICIU was one of the trouble-makers of Irish myth. An Ulster lord, he arranged a great feast to which he invited all the Ulster heroes, and ordered that the hero's portion be given to the greatest among them. At which point the three great warriors, *CUCHULAINN, CONALL* and Laoghaire, sprang up at once and began fighting each other for the honour. In order to settle the argument it was agreed that a monster should be summoned to test the courage of the three heroes. Briciu did this by challenging each one to cut off the demon's head, on the understanding that the following day that man should then lay his own head on the block. Cuchulainn stepped up first and beheaded the monster, whereupon the creature rose, took up its head and departed. The next day Cuchulainn offered his own head and the monster pronounced him the bravest man in Ireland.

BRIDE see *BRIGID*

BRIGANTIA ("High One" or "Queen") was the chief goddess of the Brigantes, the dominant tribe in the north of England before the invasion of the Romans. She was associated with water, war and healing, and also with prosperity. A widely revered goddess, she was worshipped throughout the Celtic world. In Ireland she was known as *BRIGID* and in France as Brigindo.

BRIGID, sometimes known as Brigit, was a goddess of healing and fertility who was believed to assist women in labour. She seems to have been widely worshipped in Ireland and Britain, where she was most likely known as *BRIGANTIA*. In Irish mythology, she was the wife of *BRES*, the half-*FOMORII* god who briefly led the *TUATHA DE DANANN* after the first battle of Magh Tuireadh against the *FIRBOLG*. Bres was handsome but also oppressive, like all Fomorii, so his reign was short. Brigid, however, bore him three sons. She often appears as an alternative for her mother *ANU*, which suggests that they were probably different aspects of the same mother goddess.

St Brigit, or St Bride, one of Ireland's patron saints, may have been a priestess of the goddess Brigid prior to her conversion to Christianity. It was said that she was able to feed animals without reducing the available food for the people, and this also links her with Brigid, who was celebrated at the Celtic festival of Imbolc on the first of February, at the same time as the ewes came into milk.

CAILTE, a Fenian warrior and bard, was renowned for his songs and legends. Bards or lyric poets played a central role in Celtic society, perpetuating the mysteries, praising their leaders and satirizing their enemies. Bardic schools flourished in Ireland right up to the seventeenth century. (AQUATINT BY R. HAVELL. C 1890.)

CAER was a fairy maiden who was loved by Aonghus. She chose to live as a swan for part of her life. When the swans gathered on the Lake of the Dragon's Mouth, Aonghus went to find Caer and win her love. As he reached out to her he was also turned into a swan, and they flew away together. (ILLUSTRATION BY GLENN STEWARD, 1995.)

BRIGIT see BRIGID

CAER was a fairy maiden loved by *AONGHUS*, the Irish love god. Her father Ethal was one of the *TUATHA DE DANANN*. Aonghus became aware of Caer in a dream and so attracted was he to her beauty that he fell into a deep sickness. When the identity of Caer was discovered, Aonghus immediately asked her father for her hand, but Ethal said it was not in his power to grant this because his daughter had taken the form of a swan. It was agreed, however, that Aonghus could ask Caer to marry him but only if he was able to recognize her from among the large flock of swans with whom she lived.

When the swans arrived at the Lake of the Dragon's Mouth, Aonghus went to the shore and, recognizing Caer, called out her name. Afterwards Aonghus and Caer were married.

CAMELOT, a mythical castle-city named after Camulos, was the heart of Arthur's kingdom, the seat of his power, symbol of his golden age and his most beloved home. Its shining towers drew knights from all over the world. Part of the mystique of Camelot is its elusive location which has yet to be found. (ILLUSTRATION BY ALAN LEE, 1984.)

CAILTE, son of *RONAN*, was a Fenian warrior and poet, and a cousin of *FINN MACCOOL*, leader of the *FIANNA*, the warrior bodyguard of the High King of Ireland. Cailte, though exceptionally thin, was a formidable fighter and is credited with killing *LIR*, the sea god who was the father of *MANANNAN MAC LIR*. But it was as a poet that he was most admired, and his most famous audience was St Patrick. Possibly after returning from an otherworld, Cailte was said to have travelled through Ireland recounting to the saint the legends of the hills, woods and lakes that they encountered, and also the great exploits and battles of the Fianna.

CALATIN, in Irish mythology, was a misshapen druid of *FOMORII* origin who was said to have studied sorcery for seventeen years. Queen *MEDB* of Connacht dispatched Calatin along with his numerous sons to fight the Ulster hero *CUCHULAINN*. All of them had their left hands and right feet missing, but they never missed with their poisoned spears, and Cuchulainn only succeeded in beating them with the assistance of a Connacht warrior who disapproved of such a one-sided contest. The destruction of the male Calatins did not spell the end of Cuchulainn's troubles, however, for not long afterwards Calatin's wife gave birth to three daughters, who were blinded in one eye, like the Germanic god Odin, so as to learn the magic arts. Soon the three Calatin sisters became powerful witches, and they deceived Cuchulainn with their spells, and so assisted Queen Medb's invasion of Ulster. When Cuchulainn rode out in his chariot against the invaders, he came across these hideous women cooking a dog next to the road. Either because the dog was his namesake, or because it would have been discourteous to refuse a piece of the cooked meat, Cuchulainn stopped and took hold of the dog's shoulder. As a result, his own hand and shoulder withered. Gravely weakened, he still advanced with his faithful charioteer *LAEG*.

CAMELOT see HEROIC QUESTS

CAMULOS was the god of the Remi, a Celtic tribe living in what is now Belgium, although there is evidence that he was also worshipped as a divinity of war in northern Britain and at the town of Camulodunum ("The Fort of Camulos"), modern Colchester, in Essex. The name of the town formed the basis for the mythical city of Camelot. The Romans associated Camulos with their god Mars. He was said to wield an invincible sword.

CARADAWC, in Welsh mythology, was the son of *BRAN* (son of the sea god, Llyr). When Bran sailed with his army to Ireland to avenge the ill-treatment of his sister *BRANWEN* by the High King *MATHOLWCH*, he left Caradawc as chief steward. When news of Bran's death arrived, Caradawc was overthrown by Caswallon, son of the death god Beli.

CARBONEK see CELTIC OTHERWORLDS

CATHBAD (above), *the inspired druid and seer, predicted Deirdre's tragic destiny at her birth. Druids, both male and female, held high rank in Celtic society. They were counsellors, judges, teachers and ambassadors. Even a high king could not speak at an assembly before his druid.* (ILLUSTRATION BY NICK BEALE, 1995.)

CATHBAD, in Irish mythology, was a seer and druid, and advisor to *CONCHOBHAR MAC NESSA*, the king of Ulster. Cathbad prophesied that though *DEIRDRE* would have great beauty she would bring destruction to Ulster. He also foretold that the hero *CUCHULAINN* would have a glorious but short life. When King Conchobhar Mac Nessa became cruel towards the end of his reign, Cathbad cursed the king and his stronghold at Emain Macha. Cathbad had three children, *DECHTIRE*, the mother of Cuchulainn, Elbha, the mother of *NAOISE*, and Findchaem, mother of *CONALL* Cearnach.

CERIDWEN was a Welsh goddess of fertility and the mother of Afagddu, reputedly the ugliest man in the world. To compensate for his looks Ceridwen boiled a cauldron of knowledge for a year and a day so that Afagddu could become wise and respected, and she set Gwion Bach, the second son, to watch over the pot. But Afagddu was denied the prophetic gift when a drop fell on Gwion Bach's finger and he unthinkingly sucked it. In fury, Ceridwen chased and ate Gwion Bach, only later to reincarnate him as *TALIESIN*, who was the greatest of all the Welsh bards. Ceridwen had another equally ugly son, Morfan, who was also a fearsome warrior. He fought with King

CERIDWEN boils a magical brew hoping to endow her ill-favoured son with wisdom. At the end of a year, the broth would yield just three precious drops of inspiration; but these splashed on to the hand of Gwion Bach, who became all-knowing. (ILLUSTRATION BY JAMES ALEXANDER, 1995.)

ARTHUR in his last battle, at Camlan. At first none of Sir *MODRED*'s men would fight Morfan because they thought he was ugly enough to be a devil.

CERNUNNOS was a Celtic god worshipped in both France and Britain. He is usually depicted sitting cross-legged and wearing a sleeveless tunic and bead necklace. He has an impressive pair of antlers, and the name Cernunnos means "the Horned One", which suggests that he was a god of wild animals and the forest, although he has also been seen as a god of plenty. The Romans identified him with their god Mercury, the messenger god and the guide of the dead to the underworld. In medieval Ireland the antlers of Cernunnos were transferred to the Devil.

CESAIR was the daughter of Bith, son of Noah and one of the earliest arrivals in Ireland. In her myth, Celtic and Hebrew traditions were brought somewhat uncomfortably together by the monks who wrote down the sagas and who suggested that the first settlers had reached Ireland before the Flood. Although Bith was denied a place in the Ark, he was fortunate to be advised by a god to build his own boat. Cesair appears to have guided him to this decision as well. They sailed for seven years and eventually reached

CESAIR, granddaughter of Noah, set sail with her father, Bith, to escape the Flood. After a seven-year voyage, they reached the shores of Ireland. Yet neither Cesair nor her father survived the Flood when it engulfed the land, although her husband, Fintan, escaped by changing into a salmon. (ILLUSTRATION BY JAMES ALEXANDER, 1995.)

CERNUNNOS, *a Celtic hunter god of beasts, is typically depicted in a lotus position. The "horned one" was a lord of animals and is here surrounded by wild creatures such as the stag, boar and lion. In one hand he clasps a warrior's torc, in the other a serpent, demonstrating his power.* (GUNDESTRUP CAULDRON, GILDED SILVER, C. 100 BC.)

Ireland, where Cesair was married to *FINTAN*. When the rising waters of the Flood engulfed the land, Fintan saved himself by changing into a salmon, but the rest of Bith's family drowned. This myth is known as the first invasion of Ireland. Subsequent invasions were by the *PARTHOLON* and Nemed, the *FOMORII* and *TUATHA DE DANANN*, who were all more or less supernatural in nature. The final invasion of Ireland was by the sons of *MILESIUS*, who came from Spain and brought human rule to the island.

CLIODHNA, in Irish mythology, was an otherworld goddess of beauty. It was said that her three magical birds could sing the sick to sleep and cure them. Cliodhna was passionately in love with a mortal named Ciabhan, a youth with wonderful curling locks. One day on the shore near Cork, while Ciabhan went hunting inland, Cliodhna was put into a magic sleep by the sea god *MANANNAN MAC LIR*, who then sent a wave to pull her back to the Land of Promise.

CONAIRE MOR was a High King of Ireland. He was the son of a cowherd's foster-daughter named Mess Buachalla and the bird god *NEMGLAN*. His mother was actually

the daughter of Etain Oig and *CORMAC* king of Ulster. However, Cormac was so disappointed not to have a son that he ordered Mess Buachalla to be thrown into a pit. According to the myth, the baby girl was saved by two kind-hearted servants, who could not bring themselves to carry out the king's order. Instead they gave Mess Buachalla to a cowherd. When she grew up, her beauty was so remarkable that Eterscel, the High King of Ireland, decided to marry her. He was also persuaded by a prophecy which said that an obscure woman would bear him a famous son. But on the night before the wedding, Mess Buachalla slept with the god Nemglan, who had magnificent plumage. From this union was born Conaire Mor, whom Mess Buachalla passed off as the son of Eterscel. The one instruction that Nemglan told Mess Buachalla to give to their child was that he was never to kill a bird.

When Conaire Mor was a young man, Eterscel died and the right of succession was raised in Tara, the Irish capital. It was agreed to follow the ancient custom of the dream. After a feast, one of the court would have a spell of truth sung over him as he slept. The man the courtier dreamed about would then be the next High King. In the succession dream a naked man was revealed, walking along the road to Tara with a sling in his hand.

At this time Conaire Mor was some distance from Tara. As he headed back to the palace in his chariot, a flock of birds descended upon him. They had such wonderful plumage that Conaire Mor forgot the taboo about killing birds and got out his sling. The birds shed their feathers and attacked the charioteer as warriors. But one of the birdlike fighters, who was more handsome than the rest, protected Conaire Mor. He introduced himself as his father Nemglan and reminded the young man that he must never cast stones at birds for they were his own kin. As a penance, Nemglan told his son to walk naked along the road to Tara, carrying only his sling. If he did this, and promised to rule Ireland in peace, Conaire Mor would be made High King.

So it was that Conaire Mor was received at Tara as the High King. Peace and prosperity at first marked his reign, although the lure of plunder gradually drew the Irish back to their old habit of cattle-raiding. Since Conaire Mor was reluctant to punish severely those who took

CLIODHNA *fled to Glandore to live with her mortal lover, Ciabhan, but the sea god, Manannan Mac Lir, sent a great wave to scoop her up and bring her home. Here, lulled to sleep by fairy music, she drifts back to fairyland. The Wave of Cliodhna is still one of the three great waves of Ireland.* (ILLUSTRATION BY JAMES ALEXANDER, 1995.)

CONAIRE MOR *was burdened by more geis (taboos) than any other Irish warlord. Violation of geis led to misfortune or death and marked a tragic turning-point in the hero's life. Despite his wisdom, Conaire Mor was lured by his enemies into breaking his geis one by one.* (ILLUSTRATION BY STEPHEN REID, 1910.)

part in the growing disorder, the country soon slid back into clan warfare. Eventually, the High King had to forgo the ways of peace and break his promise to his father. Conaire Mor soon realized that this would bring about his own downfall. While on campaign, he came to a roadside hostel where he was greeted by three strange horsemen, whose clothes, weapons, bodies and horses were all red. A hideous old woman told Conaire Mor that during his stay in the hostel "neither skin nor flesh of you will escape from the place to which you have come, save what the birds will take in their claws." The same night a rebel force surrounded the hostel and attacked. Three times the building caught fire and three times the flames were brought under control, but all the water had now been used. When a druid accompanying the rebels laid a spell of thirst on the High King, he sent one of his companions to fetch some water. On returning, the warrior saw that the fight was over and Conaire Mor's severed head lay on the floor. So he poured the water into the king's head, at which Conaire Mor's decapitated head praised him for his sense of duty.

SAGES AND SEERS

THE SPIRITUAL SEERS and shamans of Celtic myth were endowed with extraordinary gifts of prophecy, wisdom and healing. They enjoyed a profound rapport with natural and supernatural forces, and acted as intermediaries between the realms of the living and the dead, between the visible world of men and the invisible otherworld, a realm of wondrous spirits. Most famous of all was Arthur's wise counsellor, Merlin; but other inspired druids – Amairgen, Taliesin and Cathbad – feature in Celtic myths as prophetic bards and counsellors to clan chiefs and kings. Some lived as hermits in the wilderness, while remaining powerful in Celtic society. Although on the whole helpful to mortals, some dark sorceresses, such as Morgan, Nimue or the Calatins, used their supernatural gifts to bewitch and manipulate mortals for their own ends.

MORGAN LE FAY (above right), Queen of Avalon, the otherworldly Isle of Apples, bears an apple bough, the Celtic symbol of peace and plenty. A gifted sorceress, she is often portrayed as a dark soul, thwarting Arthur and manipulating heroes. At a deeper level, she is a winter goddess of darkness and death, opposing Arthur, the Lord of Summer. She reveals the redeeming aspect of her character in her role as sovereign healer of Avalon and guardian of Arthur's body in death. (ILLUSTRATION BY STUART LITTLEJOHN, 1994.)

MERLIN (right) is best remembered as the fatherly and spiritual guardian of Arthur. A wise seer, Merlin counselled the young king, sometimes sternly and sometimes gently, but always with wisdom. Merlin was also a peerless sage, credited with the design of the Round Table, the plan for Camelot and the stone ring at Stonehenge. He learnt his craft from a master, Bleise, portrayed here as an historian recording the deeds of Arthur's reign, as reported by Merlin. (MANUSCRIPT ILLUSTRATION, C. 1300.)

HELLAWES (*below*) *was a sorceress in the Arthurian myths who had set her heart on the noble knight Sir Lancelot, whom she had loved from afar for some seven years. Eventually, she managed to lure him into her Chapel Perilous and there she tried all the methods she knew to inspire his love for her. But it was to no avail because the steadfast and loyal knight loved one woman only, Arthur's queen, the fair Guinevere, and he had come to the chapel with but one mission in mind, which was to collect healing talismans for the wounded knight Sir Meliot. When Lancelot left with the talismans, he was completely untouched by Hellawes' love and even her magical craft. The sorceress finally realized that he would never love her and she died of a broken heart.* (ILLUSTRATION BY AUBREY BEARDSLEY, C. 1870.)

DRUIDS (*above*) *held both political and spiritual power in Celtic society and were gifted not only as shamans and seers but also as legal and moral advisors. Druids underwent a long apprenticeship of at least twenty years, learning the mysteries and laws by heart. Here, druids on a snowy hill celebrate the winter solstice by gathering a bough of mistletoe, cut with the sacred golden sickle borne by the foremost druid.* (THE DRUIDS BRINGING IN THE MISTLETOE BY G HENRY AND E A HORNED, CANVAS, 1890.)

TALIESIN (*left*), *a prophetic poet and shamanistic seer, was gifted with all-seeing wisdom after consuming a "greal" of inspiration from Ceridwen's cauldron. Wales's greatest bard, he foretold the coming of the Saxons and the oppression of the Cymry as well as his own death. He appears here as an eagle, the bird often chosen by shamans on their spirit-flights or trance journeys to the otherworld. The eagle's gold nimbus symbolizes Taliesin's radiant brow.* (ILLUSTRATION BY STUART LITTLEJOHN, 1994.)

SIR. LAVNCELOT. AND. THE. WITCH. HELLAWES.

CONALL, in Irish mythology, was the foster-brother of the Ulster hero *CUCHULAINN*. As children, they swore that if either was killed first the other would avenge him. When Queen *MEDB* of Connacht invaded Ulster, Cuchulainn faced her army single-handed, but he was doomed because he had offended the war goddess *MORRIGAN*. After Cuchulainn had been killed, and his head and sword-hand cut off by the enemy, the warriors of Ulster were stirred by Conall to wreak bloody revenge. They caught up with Queen Medb's army and Conall slew those who had killed his foster-brother. Later, Conall went on to ravage the whole of Ireland as he punished Queen Medb's allies one by one. In doing so he earned his title, Caernach ("of the Victories").

CONCHOBHAR MAC NESSA,

in Irish mythology, was an Ulster king. He was the son of Fachtna Fathach and *NESSA*, a local beauty who, according to one tradition, conceived Conchobhar on the eve

CONCHOBHAR MAC NESSA, a high king of Ireland, granted arms to the young Cuchulainn, but when the boy grasped his spears, they splintered in his hand; next, a chariot shattered beneath his stamp. No weapons withstood the hero's mighty grasp until he was given the king's own arms. (ILLUSTRATION BY STEPHEN REID, 1910.)

CONALL of the Victories, a veteran warlord, avenged Cuchulainn's death by slaying his killers one by one. From the brain of one of his victims, Mac Da Tho, he made a magic brain ball, a lethal weapon. Conall here is welcomed by his Ulstermen at a feast in Mac Da Tho's dun. (ILLUSTRATION BY STEPHEN REID, 1910.)

of her royal marriage through a secret affair with a druid. When her husband died shortly after the wedding, Nessa was courted by his half-brother and successor, *FERGUS MAC ROTH*. But she would only agree to become his wife on the condition that he would first let her son Conchobhar rule as king of Ulster for a year. An ambitious and determined woman, Nessa instructed her son how to be a great ruler so that when the time arrived for Fergus Mac Roth to return to the throne, the people of Ulster simply refused to let Conchobhar step down.

Although he was married, King Conchobhar fell deeply in love with *DEIRDRE*, who was sometimes called Derdriu ("of the Sorrows"). She was the daughter of an Ulster chieftain, and at her birth the druid *CATHBAD* had warned that, though Deirdre would be the most beautiful woman in Ireland and would marry a king, she would be the cause of death and destruction throughout the land. By the time Deirdre grew up, Conchobhar was an old man, and she in disgust

refused his advances and eloped with a handsome young warrior named *NAOISE*. But the king never gave up his passion, and so eventually he had Naoise killed and was married to Deirdre. She found her situation so intolerable that she committed suicide by throwing herself from a speeding chariot. Fergus Mac Roth, appalled by Conchobhar's behaviour, offered his services to Ulster's enemies and a long war ensued. Conchobhar was himself killed by a magic slingshot. It was the famous "brain ball" made by Conall out of the brains of a slain Leinster king. The ball lodged in the king's skull, and his doctors advised him to avoid any strenuous exercise and excitement. Some years later Conchobhar Mac Nessa got into a rage and the "brain ball" caused his death.

CONLAI, sometimes known as Connla, was the doomed son of the great Ulster hero *CUCHULAINN*. According to one Irish tradition, Cuchulainn had visited the Land of Shadows in order to challenge the warrior woman *AOIFA* to single combat. After the fight, which the

hero just managed to win by the use of cunning, they became lovers and Conlai was conceived. When he left, Cuchulainn gave Aoifa a gold ring. Years later Conlai wore this ring on a visit to Ulster, where he challenged the local heroes to combat. Just like his father, Conlai was quick to anger and soon overcame *CONALL*, Cuchulainn's foster-brother. Despite the misgivings of his wife *EMER*, Cuchulainn could not resist fighting the young stranger himself. Too proud to announce his own identity when challenged by Cuchulainn, Conlai accepted the possibility of death and drew his sword. Although Cuchulainn was impressed by sword-play that matched his own, he lost his temper the moment Conlai cut off one of his locks of hair. The terrible combat only

CONLAI, the ill-starred son of Aoifa and Cuchulainn, grew up in Skye, a stranger to his father. When he went to Ulster to challenge the local heroes, he met Cuchulainn in single combat and was killed. Recognizing his son too late, Cuchulainn was overwhelmed with grief. (ILLUSTRATION BY JAMES ALEXANDER, 1995.)

ended when Cuchulainn drove his spear through Conlai's stomach. Only then did Cuchulainn notice on his young opponent's finger the gold ring he had given to Aoifa. Cuchulainn, overwhelmed with remorse and grief, carried the dying Conlai to his house and afterwards buried his forgotten son.

CORMAC was the son of the Ulster king *CONCHOBHAR MAC NESSA*. An Irish myth tells of his distaste at his father's treachery in killing *NAOISE*, the husband of *DEIRDRE*, and of his going into voluntary exile with the deposed Ulster ruler *FERGUS MAC ROTH*. Not until he received an invitation from his father Conchobhar, when the dying king had nominated Cormac as his successor, did he consider returning home. However, a druidess had warned Cormac that if he went back to Ulster he would be killed, but he set out anyway and on the journey he fell into a deep magic sleep and was slain by a group of warriors. The attack was said to have been arranged by a jealous husband, whose wife had fallen in love with Cormac.

CORMAC (below), returning home after his long, voluntary exile, stopped by a roadside hostel where he was lulled to sleep by the soft notes of a harp. Defenceless in his enchanted sleep, he was slain by assassins, sent by the harpist, Craiftine, in revenge for Cormac's affair with his wife. (ILLUSTRATION BY NICK BEALE, 1995.)

CORMAC MAC ART'S (above) reign was distinguished by peace and plenty. A wise and good man, he was favoured by the Tuatha De Danann who invited him to their hidden world, and gave him a curative apple branch. In tune with Christian kindness, he warmly welcomed St Patrick at his court. (ILLUSTRATION BY JAMES ALEXANDER 1995.)

CORMAC MAC ART was the High King of Ireland during the period that *FINN MACCOOL* led the Fenian warrior band. He was the most famous of the early rulers of Ireland, his reign being tentatively dated from 227 to 266. Cormac Mac Art was the Irish Solomon, a wise and powerful king, who was well served by the brave exploits of Finn MacCool. His wisdom seems to have impressed the *TUATHA DE DANANN*. These gods and goddesses invited Cormac Mac Art to their home in the otherworld, where they gave him wonderful presents. One of these was a silver branch that bore golden apples, and when shaken produced music that could cure the sick and wounded. On his own death Cormac Mac Art had to hand back this incredible talisman. One of Cormac's sons, Cellach, raped the niece of Aonghus of the Terrible Spear. In the ensuing fight, Cellach was slain and Cormac lost an eye. As a High King could have no imperfection Cormac had to step down and his son Cairbe took his place. The reputation of the High King remained so strong that later the Irish Christians also adopted him. It was claimed that Cormac Mac Art learned of the Christian faith before it was actually preached in Ireland by St Patrick, with the result that he ordered that he should not be buried at the royal cemetery by the River Boyne because of its pagan associations.

CREIDHNE was the goldsmith of the *TUATHA DE DANANN* and the brother of *GOIBHNIU*, the smith god, and Luchtar, the carpenter. During the second battle of Magh Tuireadh, when the De Danann finally defeated the *FOMORII*, the three brothers could be seen on the battlefield making and repairing spears with magical speed. As Goibhniu fashioned a blade with three blows of his hammer, Luchtar carved a handle in a flash, and Creidhne crafted rivets that flew into place and bonded at once.

CUCHULAINN as a youngster lived at the court of the High King, where he trained with other sons of chieftains, whom he soon outstripped in arms and might. Although small, he glowed with an inner divine light and warmth, which he inherited from his father the sun god Lugh.

(ILLUSTRATION BY STEPHEN REID, 1912.)

CUCHULAINN, in Irish mythology, was the champion warrior of Ulster. His name means "the Hound of Culann", although he was usually called the Hound of Ulster. Cuchulainn was the Irish Achilles, a larger-than-life fighter whose bouts of temper often caused grief to himself and others. Anger certainly made him slay his son *CONLAI*, when the young man travelled from the Land of Shadows to visit Ulster. The fifteen-year-old warrior was Cuchulainn's son by the warrior-princess *AOIFA*. Neither father nor son would identify themselves, so a tragic fight ensued. A gold ring on Conlai's finger revealed too late that he was Cuchulainn's own offpsring.

Cuchulainn's mother was *DECHTIRE*, the daughter of the druid *CATHBAD*, an advisor to the King *CONCHOBHAR MAC NESSA*. It was Cathbad who foretold that Cuchulainn would become a great warrior but die young. Shortly after her marriage to *SUALTAM MAC ROTH*, who was the brother of the deposed Ulster ruler *FERGUS MAC ROTH*, Dechtire along with fifty of her kinswomen flew to the otherworld in the form of a flock of birds. During the wedding feast she had swallowed a fly and dreamed as a result of the sun god *LUGH*, who told her to make this journey. Cathbad reassured his son-in-law by saying that Dechtire had merely gone to visit her otherworld relations, for her mother was a daughter of the god *AONGHUS*. In fact, Lugh kept Dechtire there for his own pleasure for three years.

When Dechtire and her women returned to Emain Macha, the stronghold of the Ulster kings, in the form of brightly coloured birds, Dechtire was expecting Lugh's son, Setanta. Sualtam Mac Roth was so pleased to have his wife home again that when the boy was born he accepted him as his own child.

As a youth, Setanta quickly learned the ways of the warrior, but it was not obvious to everyone just how strong and brave he was until he killed an enormous hound with his bare hands. One day, arriving late at the gate of a house where King Cochobhar Mac Nessa was being entertained by the Ulster smith *CULANN*, the young hero was attacked by the ferocious guard dog and only saved himself by dashing out its brains on one of the gate's pillars. Their host had now lost a faithful guardian, so Setanta offered to take the hound's place while a replacement was found. When Culann thanked the young warrior but declined his offer, it was decided that henceforth Setanta would be known as Cuchulainn ("the Hound of Culann").

Even though Cathbad warned that anyone going to battle for the first time on a certain day was destined for a short life, Cuchulainn could not wait to deal with Ulster's enemies and he soon took up arms against three semi-divine warriors named Foill, Fannell and Tuachell, as well as their numerous followers, all of whom he killed. In this combat Cuchulainn displayed for the first time the dreadful shape of his battle-frenzy. His body trembled violently; his heels and calves appeared in front; one eye receded into his head, the other stood out huge and red on his cheek; a man's head could fit into his jaw; his hair bristled like hawthorn, with a drop of blood at the end of each single hair; and from the top of his head arose a thick column of dark blood like the mast of a ship. Returning to Emain Macha in his chariot, "graced with the bleeding heads of his enemies", and with the battle-frenzy still upon him, Cuchulainn was only stopped from circling the defences and screaming for a fight through a ploy of the Ulster queen Mughain. She led out of Emain Macha some hundred and fifty naked women carrying three vats of cold water. An embarrassed or amazed Cuchulainn was swiftly womanhandled into the vats. The first one burst its sides. The second boiled furiously, but the last vat became only very hot. Thus was the young hero tamed after his first taste of blood.

In his calm, everyday state of mind Cuchulainn was a favourite of womenfolk. But he fell in love with *EMER*, the daughter of Fogall, a wily chieftain whose castle was close to Dublin. Cuchulainn asked for Emer's hand but Fogall, who was against the match, pointed out that Cuchulainn had yet to establish his reputation as a warrior and suggested that he should go and learn

CUCHULAINN, the Irish Achilles, performed many mighty deeds in his brief years. The hero's dreamy eyes reflect his idealism, which is expressed in the inscription beneath this portrait, "I care not though I last but a day if my name and my fame are a power forever."

(CUCHULAINN BY JOHN DUNCAN, CANVAS, 1913.)

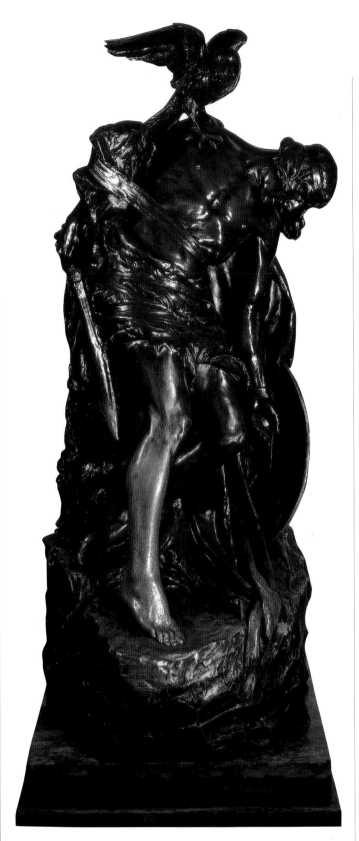

For a year and a day Cuchulainn was taught by Scathach, and became the lover of her daughter *UATHACH*. Scathach seems to have feared for the safety of Cuchulainn, and she warned him without success not to challenge her sister Aoifa. But Cuchulainn beat Aoifa by cunning, and afterwards she became his mistress, conceiving the unfortunate Conlai. Cuchulainn finally returned to Fogall's stronghold and claimed Emer, but only after a heated battle with Fogall and his warriors, during which Fogall leapt to his death escaping the hero.

Acclaimed as the champion of Ireland in a beheading contest, Cuchulainn was soon unbeatable in combat, a skill he was to need dearly in his last campaign, which was a single-handed defence of Ulster against the invading army of Queen *MEDB* of Connacht. The main reason for this large-scale cattle raid was a famous brown bull which was kept in Cuailgne. But the tyrannical ruler of Ulster, King Conchobhar Mac Nessa, also played a part in gathering rebellious Ulstermen and others from many parts of Ireland to Queen Medb's side. One prophecy told the queen that there would be "crimson and red" upon her forces because of Cuchulainn's prowess, but she was determined to invade and she also had three advantages. First, the great hero had made bitter enemies of the *CALATIN* family, whose daughters were witches. Just prior to his last stand along with his faithful charioteer *LAEG*, they cast a spell on Cuchulainn which withered a shoulder and a hand. Second, Medb attacked when Ulster's heroes were laid low by *MACHA*'s curse, and were unable to fight for five days and nights. Finally, Cuchulainn had lost the support of the goddess *MORRIGAN*, because he had rejected her passionate advances. Yet he still managed to conduct a successful single-handed defence and was able to slow the advance of Queen

CUCHULAINN journeyed to the Isle of Skye to train in the martial arts. On the Isle he met a man who gave him a flaming wheel to guide him through the deadly quagmire. The guide was his father, the sun god, Lugh. (ILLUSTRATION BY STEPHEN REID, 1912.)

Medb's forces by the use of clever tactics and lightning attacks, until the effects of Macha's curse had almost worn off, and the dazed warriors were able to respond to Sualtam Mac Roth's call to arms. But their help came too late for Cuchulainn. Pressed on all sides by his enemies, the Ulster champion was overcome in spite of aid from his divine father, the sun god Lugh. His only companion, Laeg, was laid low with a spear, then Cuchulainn himself suffered a terrible stomach wound that even Lugh could not heal. Finally, Cuchulainn tied himself to an upright stone in order to fight till his last breath. As soon as he died Morrigan, in the form of a crow, settled on his shoulder and his enemies cut off his head and right hand, leaving his body for the carrion birds. Conall, his foster-brother, managed to recover the missing parts, but Ulster wept for the loss of their champion. Indeed, so widespread was Cuchulainn's fame that his exploits influenced the development of the Arthurian myths in Britain and France. (See also *MAGIC AND ENCHANTMENT; CELTIC ROMANCE*)

CUCHULAINN, mortally wounded in his final combat but determined to fight to the end, lashed himself to a pillar and died on his feet. At the end a crow settled on his shoulder, signifying death. This memorial symbolizes all those who fought for Irish independence. (THE DEATH OF CUCHULAINN BY O SHEPPARD, BRONZE, 1916.)

from the Scottish champion Domhall. Domhall told Cuchulainn that his best trainer in arms would be *SCATHACH*, a warrior-princess in the Land of Shadows. So he travelled to this mysterious land and served Scathach. She taught the young hero his famous battle leap.

CULANN, in Irish mythology, was an Ulster smith who was thought to be a reincarnation of the sea god *MANANNAN MAC LIR*. It was his enormous guardian dog that young Setanta killed with his bare hands. Culann was angry about this so Setanta offered to become his hound until a new one was trained. Thereafter the young man was known as *CUCHULAINN*, "the Hound of Culann".

CULHWCH, in Welsh mythology, was the son of Cildydd, one of King *ARTHUR*'s knights. His stepmother hated Culhwch so much that she placed a curse on him that he could marry only *OLWEN*, the daughter of the giant Yspaddaden. This fate, however, seemed less dreadful once Culhwch found Olwen, a task which took over a year, for they fell deeply in love. Culhwch's next problem was how to persuade her giant father to agree to the match. Like the Irish Cyclops *BALOR*, Yspaddaden's eyelids needed to be levered up with supports in order for him to see

CULANN (below), the Ulster smith, and the High King Conchobhar gaze in amazement at the young Cuchulainn who slew Culann's fierce hound outright when the great guard dog had attacked the hero at the gate. To compensate for killing his hound, Cuchulainn offered to take its place. (ILLUSTRATION BY STEPHEN REID, 1912.)

CU ROI and his comrade, Cuchulainn, on one wild escapade, raided Inis Ter Falga, carrying off the king's booty and beautiful daughter, Blathnat. When the heroes fell out over the girl, Cuchulainn was at one point beaten and buried up to his arms while Cu Roi galloped off with Blathnat. (ILLUSTRATION BY JAMES ALEXANDER, 1995.)

Culhwch. Also like Balor, the Welsh giant did not favour the idea of his daughter marrying a man. At interviews held on successive days Yspaddaden threw a poisoned spear at Culhwch and his companions, but they managed on each occasion to catch it and throw it back. When Culhwch finally put out one of the giant's eyes with a return throw, Yspaddaden agreed to the marriage on condition that Culhwch perform a whole series of difficult tasks. With the assistance of King Arthur's men and a couple of divine allies, Culhwch successfully completed these trials, then killed Yspaddaden and married Olwen. (See also *HEROIC QUESTS*)

CUMAL (whose name means "sky") was the father of the Fenian hero Finn Mac Cumal, more commonly known as *FINN MACCOOL*, who was born after his father's death. Cumal was also a renowned leader of the *FIANNA* and chief of the Clan Bascna. He was killed by Jadhg, a druid, who had been enraged when Cumal eloped with his daughter.

CU ROI (whose name means "hound of Roi") was a Munster king. It was King Cu Roi who transformed himself into *UATH*, the dreadful giant, in order to choose the champion of Ireland. The three

CULHWCH (right), on his quest for Olwen, arrives at Arthur's court, seeking help and counsel. This Victorian painting evokes a medieval mood, portraying the hero as a courtly hunter from the Age of Chivalry. The surly steward could be Arthur's brusque seneschal, Kay. (KILHWYCH, THE KING'S SON BY ARTHUR GASKIN, WOOD, C. 1900.)

contenders for the championship – Laoghaire, Cuchulainn's foster-brother CONALL, and CUCHULAINN himself – were invited by Cu Roi to a beheading contest, which only Cuchulainn had enough courage to go through with. Later, Cu Roi and Cuchulainn carried off BLATHNAT, a beautiful woman. Although she expressed her love for Cuchulainn, Cu Roi took her to his castle in Munster. When Cuchulainn laid siege to the stronghold, Blathnat betrayed Cu Roi by showing how the place could be entered.

CYNON, according to a late Arthurian myth, was a knight who encountered a black man with one foot and one eye, and bearing a large wooden club. This Fomorii-like fighter, doubtless a cousin of the violent and misshapen Irish sea gods, ordered Cynon to go to a fountain and fill with water a silver bowl that he would find there , and then to throw the water against a marble slab. Sir Cynon did as he was instructed and a Black Knight appeared to the sound of thunder and the singing of magic birds. Sir

CYNON, an Arthurian hero, battles with the Black Knight, a mysterious warrior who appeared by magic. Although defeated, Cynon returned home on foot to tell the tale, and thus inspired Owain to set out on his memorable quest. Years later Cynon retraced his steps in search of Owain. (ILLUSTRATION BY H THEAKER, 1920.)

Cynon then fought his mysterious opponent but was defeated.

DAGDA means "the good god". He was in fact the great god of Irish mythology, and was usually depicted as a man in rustic clothes dragging an enormous club on wheels. With one end of this weapon he could slay his enemies and with the other he could restore the dead to life. Dagda was believed to be wise, full of knowledge and well versed in the magic arts. He was a chief of the TUATHA DE DANANN.

Dagda was a great fighter and the lover of MORRIGAN, the war goddess. The bones of his enemies were described as "hailstones under horses' hooves" when he wielded his mighty club. Like an all-powerful chieftain, Dagda led the Tuatha De Danann on the battlefield, slaying all those who dared to confront him. Yet he was also associated with abundance, being able to satisfy the hunger of everybody by means of an inexhaustible cauldron. That Dagda took great pleasure in eating was apparent, when just before the second battle of Magh Tuireadh he visited the camp of the FOMORII, his bitter enemies, during a truce at the time of the New Year festival. There they made for him a porridge of milk, flour, fat, pigs and goats, enough for fifty men.

On pain of death Dagda was ordered by the Fomorii to consume this massive meal, which he readily did with a huge wooden ladle "so big that a man and a woman could have slept together in it". This test turned Dagda temporarily into a gross old man, but it did not prevent him from making love to a Fomorii girl, who promised to use her magic on behalf of the Tuatha De Danann. The story may recall, in a distorted form, a holy marriage between a chieftain and a maiden at the beginning of each year; similar to

DANA, the great mother goddess, gave her name to the Tuatha De Danann, a race of wonderful, beautiful but often vulnerable gods who lived in the sparkling otherworld. Here, they gather to hear the poignant song of Lir's children, ill-starred gods who were turned into swans. (ILLUSTRATION BY STEPHEN REID, 1912.)

DAGDA, father of the gods, owned a wondrous cauldron of plenty and a double-edged magic club, carried on wheels. This bronze relief of a powerful Celtic deity, with a wheel, is regarded by some to be Dagda, with the wheel symbolizing his treasures. (GUNDESTRUP CAULDRON, GILDED SILVER, C. 100 BC.)

the sacred rite that was performed by a Sumerian ruler and a priestess in Mesopotamia. This union was meant to ensure prosperity, strength and peace.

Although the eventual defeat of the Fomorii at the second battle of Magh Tuireadh was really due to the sun god LUGH, it was Dagda who was held in the greatest respect, even after the Tuatha De Danann were in their turn overthrown by the sons of MILESIUS, the ancestors of the present-day Irish.

To Dagda fell the important task of settling the defeated Tuatha De Danann underground. Just as the Fomorii had retreated beneath the waves, so the vanquished De Danann disappeared underground. Over the centuries these powerful deities were gradually transformed into fairies – the *bean sidhe* or BANSHEES of Irish folklore. (See also WONDROUS CAULDRONS)

DANA, another name for ANU, was the goddess after whom the TUATHA DE DANANN were named – "the people of the goddess Dana".

DECHTIRE, in Irish mythology, was the mother of *CUCHULAINN*. She was a daughter of Maga, the child of the love god *AONGHUS* and of the druid *CATHBAD*, advisor to King *CONCHOBHAR MAC NESSA* of Ulster. When Dechtire married *SUALTAM MAC ROTH*, a fly flew into her cup during the wedding feast and she swallowed it. She fell into a deep sleep and dreamed that the sun god *LUGH* insisted that she and fifty of her kinswomen follow him to the otherworld as a flock of birds. Three years later a flock of brightly coloured birds reappeared at Emain Macha, the capital of Ulster. The Ulstermen went after them with slings, but were unable to hit any of them. It was decided, therefore, to surprise·the birds at night as they rested. So it was that the warriors came upon Dechtire, her women and Lugh sleeping in a hut on a site renowned for its magical properties. When Conchobhar was told of of this he sent for Dechtire at once, but she told her captors that she was too ill to be able to travel for another day. The next morning she showed them her new-born son, a gift to Ulster.

DECHTIRE, who had disappeared mysteriously on her wedding day, returned three years later with the shining sun god, Lugh. Dechtire brought with her a gift from the otherworld – her child, Setanta, who became Ulster's greatest hero, Cuchulainn. (ILLUSTRATION BY G DENHAM, C. 1900.)

DEIRDRE grieves for the death of her beloved Naoise and his brothers, slain by the jealous King Conchobhar. Over the brothers' grave, she sang her pitiable lament, "May my heart not break today for the sea-tides of our everyday sorrows are strong, but I am sorrow itself..." (DEIRDRE OF THE SORROWS BY JOHN DUNCAN, C. 1912.)

DEIRDRE was the cause of Ulster's sorrows, according to Irish mythology. The druid *CATHBAD* foretold this before she was born, as well as telling of how beautiful she would become. When she grew up, King *CONCHOBHAR MAC NESSA* wished to marry her, even though he was already advanced in years, but Deirdre would have none of this. She persuaded *NAOISE* and his brothers to run away with her to Alba. After living for many years in their voluntary exile, they were tricked into returning to Ulster on the understanding that they would come to no harm. But Conchobhar arranged to have Naoise killed and then forced Deirdre to agree to marry him. Once married, however, Deirdre remained sad and kept her distance from the king, with the result that he handed her over to the killer of Naoise. Rather than sleep with this man, she threw herself from his speeding chariot and smashed her brains out on a rock. From each of the graves of Naoise and Deirdre grew a pine, which eventually intertwined and grew as a single tree.

DERBFORGAILLE was the daughter of a ruler of Lochlann. When her father left her on the shore as a tribute for the *FOMORII*, she was rescued by the Ulster hero *CUCHULAINN* and fell in love with him. In order to follow him, she turned herself into a swan. However, unaware of the bird's true identity, Cuchulainn brought her down with a sling-shot. She returned to human form and he sucked the stone out of the wound, but now they were linked by blood and so he could not marry her.

DIAN CECHT was the Irish god of healing. It was said that with his daughter Airmid, he had charge of a spring whose waters restored the dying gods to life. After *NUADA*, the leader of the *TUATHA DE DANANN*, lost his hand fighting the *FIRBOLG* at the first battle of Magh Tuireadh, Dian Cecht gave him a silver hand, thus earning him the title Nuada "of the Silver Hand". Impressed though the Tuatha De Danann were by Dian Cecht's handiwork, Nuada was felt to be no longer fit to be a war leader and *BRES*, who was

half *FOMORII*, took his place. But Bres was a tyrant and became very unpopular, so Nuada was restored to the leadership, once Dian Cecht's son Miach had made him a new hand of flesh and blood. Apparently the god of healing grew jealous of his son's medical skills and so killed him.

DIARMUID UA DUIBHNE, or Diarmuid "of the Love Spot", was the foster-son of the Irish love god *AONGHUS*. His mortal father gave him to the god as a child, a gift that was returned when Diarmuid received the famous love spot as a young Fenian warrior. One night, when out hunting, Diarmuid and three companions took shelter in a small hut in a wood. There a beautiful young woman received them but chose to sleep only with Diarmuid. She told him that she was Youth, and that the love spot she put on his forehead would make him irresistible to women. As a consequence, Diarmuid's life was almost continuously troubled by desperate women, the worst being *GRAINNE*, the passionate daughter of High King *CORMAC MAC ART*. Grainne was betrothed to *FINN MACCOOL*, the Fenian commander, but she wanted Diarmuid and forced him to elope with her. For sixteen years the Fenians pursued them until, at the request of the king and the love god, a peace was grudgingly made.

It seemed that Diarmuid and Grainne would settle down to a contented family life and they had several children. But Diarmuid's own destiny was about to catch up with him. His mortal father had killed his brother at birth because

he believed that Aonghus' steward, Roc, was responsible for the pregnancy. However, Roc revived the infant as a magic boar and told it to bring Diarmuid to his death. When hunting one day with Cormac Mac Art and Finn MacCool, Diarmuid came face to face with this creature. His hounds fled in terror, his slingshot had no impact on the charging boar's head and his sword broke in two, so the irresistible Diarmuid was left bleeding to death on the ground. Finn MacCool refused to fetch the dying Diarmuid a drink of water, and by the time the other hunters arrived on the scene, he was too near to death to be saved. Grainne was devastated by the loss, although she was moved by the way that Aonghus took care of Diarmuid's corpse. He took the body to his own palace by the River Boyne, where he breathed a new soul into Diarmuid so that they could converse each day. This was how the young man came to live with the TUATHA DE DANANN, who had by this time left the upper world and lived beneath the soil of Ireland.

DIARMUID, gored by a wild boar, was denied healing water by Finn, still smarting over Diarmuid's love affair with Grainne. A Celtic Adonis, the hero was loved by women often against his will, and, like Adonis, was killed by a boar, but enjoyed some form of immortality. (ILLUSTRATION BY H J FORD, 1912.)

DON was the Welsh equivalent of the Irish mother goddess DANA and was the daughter of Mathonwy, sister of MATH, and the wife of Beli, the god of death. She had many children, including AMAETHON, ARIANRHOD, Govannon, GWYDION, Gilvaethwy and NUDD.

DIAN CECHT (above), god of healing, guards the sacred spring of health with his daughter, Airmid. Its miracle waters cured the sick and restored the dead to life. Known as the father of medicine, Dian Cecht is credited with a remarkable sixth-century Brehon Law tract on the practice of medicine. (ILLUSTRATION BY NICK BEALE, 1995.)

DON (below), the Welsh mother goddess, was as popular as her Irish counterpart, Dana. This female figure, surrounded by birds and children, is widely assumed to be a Celtic mother goddess. She is one of several Celtic deities embossed on the gilded panels of the Gundestrup Cauldron. (GILDED SILVER, C. 100 BC.)

DIARMUID (below), a gifted Fenian warrior, was lured underground by the De Danann who often recruited champions to fight in their otherworldly battles. To test his skill, they sent a mysterious warrior to challenge him as he drank from their forest well. (ILLUSTRATION BY STEPHEN REID, 1912.)

MAGIC AND ENCHANTMENT

ENCHANTMENT PERMEATES Celtic myth, shrouding the tales in a haunting, dreamlike quality. The all-pervasive otherworld lies behind much of the mystery and magic, penetrating the forests and lakes, and crafting charmed rings and weapons. Yet spells and magic also arose in the visible world where bards, druids and some privileged heroes, such as Finn MacCool, possessed magical powers. Bards could weaken the enemy with satire or enchanted sleep, while druids bewitched the host with magical illusions. Off the battlefield, love and romance were also subject to spells, love philtres or magical

trickery, as in the romances of Sadb, Rhiannon and Iseult. On the brighter side, many heroes enjoyed the gifts of the otherworld, such as Arthur's sword, Excalibur, or Fergus Mac Roth's *sidhe* sword; while Fergus Mac Leda's water-shoes afforded underwater adventures; and countless heroes were nourished or reborn from magical cauldrons.

FERGUS MAC LEDA, (above), a high king of Ulster, owned a pair of water-shoes with which he enjoyed underwater travel. He never tired of exploring the depths of the lakes and rivers of Ireland until he encountered a fierce river-horse in Loch Rury. The incident so terrified Fergus that his face became permanently distorted with fear. As only an unblemished king could rule Ireland, Fergus returned to the loch to slay the monster before going down himself, but with a face at last restored and serene. (ILLUSTRATION BY STEPHEN REID, 1912.)

THE ENCHANTED FOREST (left) of Arthurian legend, was alive with beguiling fairy maidens, who often taunted errant knights. One such, La Belle Dame Sans Merci, described by the poet Keats, was a banshee who attracted mortal lovers for her own amusement, inspiring them with a hopeless infatuation and then leaving them bereft of will or purpose until they withered on the lake, "alone and palely loitering". As the languishing knight here sleeps, he dreams of the pale kings and warriors whom La Belle Dame holds in thrall. (LA BELLE DAME SANS MERCI BY H M RHEAM, CANVAS. 1897.)

EXCALIBUR (above), Arthur's enchanted sword, shone with the light of thirty torches and dazzled his enemies. The precious scabbard prevented the loss of blood in battle, but Arthur rather rashly handed this talisman over to his half-sister Morgan Le Fay for safekeeping; she instantly made a duplicate for Arthur, passing the original on to her lover, Accolon. Here, Arthur marvels at the sword rising from a white-clad arm in the enchanted lake. (ILLUSTRATION BY AUBREY BEARDSLEY, C. 1870.)

PWYLL'S (above) family wander in an enchanted wilderness after their country, Dyfed, had been spirited away in a peal of thunder. The baffling enchantment was part of a lingering curse placed on Pwyll to avenge Gwawl, a rival suitor for the hand of Rhiannon. Even after Pwyll's death, the spell blighted his family, until Rhiannon's new husband, Manawydan, struck a deal with the enchanter, who at last restored Dyfed to its former beauty. (ILLUSTRATION BY ALAN LEE, 1984)

MERLIN (right), wise and thoughtful though he was, was enchanted by the ravishing Lady of the Lake, Nimue, and despite his foresight, he allowed himself to be lured deep beneath a stone and bound there by his own magic spells. In another legend, Nimue put Merlin into a trance beneath a thorn tree and then trailed her veil around him, creating an invisible tower of air in which he was trapped forever. It is said that his voice can still be heard in the plaintive rustling of leaves. (ILLUSTRATION BY ALAN LEE, 1984.)

E

DONN ("the Dark One") was the Irish god of the dead. He is sometimes confused with *EBER* Donn, one of the leaders of the sons of *MILESIUS*, who insulted *ERIU*, one of the *TUATHA DE DANANN*, and was drowned off the south-west coast of Ireland. Donn's home, the House of Donn, was thought to be an assembly point on the journey to the otherworld.

DRUIDS see *SAGES AND SEERS*

DUBH was a druidess. According to one Irish tradition, her anger at her husband Enna's passion for another woman ultimately led to the name of Dublin. Dubh used magic to drown her rival, but her husband in turn drowned her in what became known as Dubhlinn ("Dubh's pool").

DYLAN ("Son of the Wave") was a Welsh sea god whose parents were *ARIANRHOD* and her brother *GWYDION*. As soon as he was born

DYLAN, a Welsh sea deity, leapt from his mother's arms at birth and plunged straight into the sea and swam as well as any fish. Beloved by the sea, all the waves wept when he was killed, and his death-groan can still be heard in the roar of the incoming tide. (THE BAPTISM OF DYLAN, SON OF THE WAVE BY GEORGE SHERRINGHAM, CANVAS, C. 1900.)

DONN, god of the dead, gathers souls around him as they assemble on his stormy island before setting out on their journey to the otherworld. Inevitably, he became associated in popular folklore with shipwrecks and sea storms, and was often confused with Eber Donn, who died at sea. (ILLUSTRATION BY JAMES ALEXANDER, 1995.)

he headed straight to the sea, where he immediately swam as well as a fish. When his uncle, the smith god Govannon, killed him, all the waves of Britain and Ireland lamented his death.

EBER was the name of two of the three leaders who led the Milesians in their conquest of Ireland. They were Eber Donn, or Eber "the Brown", and Eber Finn, or Eber "the Fair". The third was named Eremon. Eber Donn failed to reach the Irish coast because his ship foundered in a storm caused by, it was said, his bloody war cry. The

druid *AMAIRGEN* had only just succeeded in casting a spell over the turbulent waves, when Eber Donn was seized by a battle-frenzy and the charm was broken by his wild cries. After the defeat of the *TUATHA DE DANANN*, the advice of Amairgen was ignored by Eber Finn, who refused to acknowledge the right of his older brother Eremon to be king of the whole island. So it was that Ireland was partitioned into two kingdoms, with Eremon ruling the north and Eber Finn the south. But Eber Finn invaded Eremon's territory and laid waste to his lands until he fell in battle. Eremon then became the first High King of all Ireland.

EFNISIEN, in Welsh mythology, was the troublesome half-brother of *BRAN THE BLESSED* who caused the rift between Bran and King *MATHOLWCH*. Because Efnisien had not been consulted by Bran over the marriage of his half-sister *BRANWEN* to the Irish king, he proceeded to cut off the lips, ears and tails of Matholwch's horses during the wedding feast. To compensate for this act, Bran gave Matholwch a magic cauldron that was capable of restoring dead warriors to life, but with one small imperfection – they came back to life without the power of speech. However, the

Irish did not consider this gift a sufficient redress for Efnisien's act of mutilation, and some time after her arrival in Ireland Branwen was demoted from being queen to just a lowly cook in the palace kitchens. Efnisien accompanied the army that was sent against Matholwch to avenge this insult. It was fortunate for Bran that his half-brother did come, because Efnisien foiled a cunning trap that had been laid for the Britons by Matholwch in his hall. He had placed behind each of Bran's strongest warriors a sack hung from the wall containing an armed Irishman, and at a signal they were to fall upon the Britons during what was supposed to be a feast of welcome. When Efnisien inspected the hall beforehand, he asked what was in one of the bags. On being told it was corn, Efnisien laid hold of the sack and felt about till his fingers closed on the head of the warrior within it, then he squeezed and cracked his skull. One by one Efnisien asked about the contents of the sacks and each time repeated his squeezing.

The feast took place therefore not as Matholwch had planned. An even more unexpected turn of events occurred when Efnisien threw Matholwch's three-year-old son by Branwen on to the fire. Branwen would have leapt after her

ELATHA (above), a Fomorii king, lived beneath the waves with his violent and misshapen people. Unlike the other Fomorii, Elatha was a godlike being with long golden hair. Emerging from the sea one day in his silver ship, he met the lovely goddess, Eri, who fell immediately in love with him. Soon after, they had a handsome but troublesome son, Bres. (ILLUSTRATION BY NICK BEALE, 1995.)

EBER DONN (above) and the Milesian chiefs drift in the fairy sea mists off the Irish coast. On board Eber's ship, the druid Amairgen charmed the sea with magic of his own, but Eber let out his great war cry which broke the druid's spell and stirred up a storm in which he was drowned. (ILLUSTRATION BY JAMES ALEXANDER, 1995.)

EFNISIEN (below) inspects sacks in Matholwch's hall. In each sack he felt a warrior's head, which he crushed between his fingers. The moody trickster went on to provoke a deadly contest, but then, in remorse, sacrificed himself to save his comrades. (ILLUSTRATION BY STEPHEN REID, 1910.)

son, but Bran held her back. In the fight that took place afterwards the Britons were almost defeated by the magic cauldron that Bran had given Matholwch, because at night it restored to life the Irish warriors who had been slain during the day. The Britons were in a desperate predicament and so Efnisien, at the cost of his life, destroyed the magic cauldron. He hid among the Irish dead and was thrown into the boiling cauldron, where he stretched and burst its sides, but the great effort involved killed him.

ELATHA, in Irish mythology, was the son of Delbaeth, the leader of the *FOMORII* and father of *BRES*, who was briefly the leader of the *TUATHA DE DANANN*. Unlike the other Fomorii, who were described as being hideous and deformed, Elatha was fair and had golden hair. He met the goddess Eri on the sea shore and there they conceived their child Bres. When Bres was removed from the leadership of the De Danann, he and his mother went to Elatha to ask for help, but the Fomorii were defeated at the second battle of Magh Tuireadh and driven from Ireland.

EMER, in Irish mythology, was the daughter of Fogall and the wife of *CUCHULAINN*, who first saw her when he was at the court of the High King of Ireland at Tara. She appeared "dark-haired almost as himself, and her skin white as mare's milk, and her eyes wide and proud and brilliant like the eyes of Fedelma, his favourite falcon". Emer's father was a chieftain from Meath and was against the match. He told Cuchulainn to travel to improve his fighting skills and only then would he consider him as a son-in-law. Cuchulainn survived and returned to claim his bride. Indeed, Cuchulainn was forced to attack the reluctant Fogall's fortress before the wedding could take place. Although Emer was totally enraptured by her handsome husband, their marriage was not without its troubles, not least because many other women also found the Ulster hero attractive. Just before his final battle, when he fought the army of Queen *MEDB* alone, Emer tried to persuade him to remain in the fortress of Emain Macha, the seat of King *CONCHOBHAR MAC NESSA*. However, he got on his chariot when it was brought

around to the front of his house. Even then, he thought of Emer's request, but his enemies the witches of *CALATIN* cast a spell to harden his resolve to fight single-handed.

ENID see *CELTIC ROMANCE*

EMER, a peerless Irish maiden, inspired the love of Ulster's great hero, Cuchulainn. She was blessed with the six gifts of womanhood: beauty, chastity, wisdom, sweet speech, song and needlecraft. When the hero courted her, she smiled at his youth, and said that he had "deeds to do". (ILLUSTRATION BY STEPHEN REID, 1912.)

E

ETAIN (right), one of the High Queens of Ireland, appears with her peers in power and beauty: from left to right, Etain, Greek Helen, Medb and Fand, the fairy queen. The jewelled cup of plenty recalls Etain's links with the otherworld. (ETAIN, HELEN, MEDB AND FAND BY HARRY CLARKE, GLASS, C. 1900.)

EPONA, the Celtic horse goddess, won the favour of the Roman army and was depicted in monuments set up at its cavalry barracks as a woman riding a fast steed, her cloak billowing with air behind her. She was even given her own festival in Rome on December 18. Originally, Epona was almost certainly seen by the Celts as a mare, possibly like the great white horse carved in the chalk downs near Wantage, in southern England. The fact that she is often depicted riding a horse with a foal suggests that she was also a goddess of fertility. In the Welsh myth of *PWYLL* there is a connection between Epona and his wife *RHIANNON*, who is made to carry visitors into her husband's palace.

ERIU, or Erinn, was the wife of Ma Greine, son of *OGMA*, and herself one of the *TUATHA DE DANANN*. When the Milesians invaded, she and her two sisters, Banba and

EPONA (below), the Celtic horse goddess, was adopted by the Roman cavalry who spread her cult across Europe. Her effigy, often placed in stables, portrayed her riding side-saddle, sometimes with a foal, which reflected her role as a fertility goddess, symbolized here by the wheat and birds. (ILLUSTRATION BY MIRANDA GRAY, 1995.)

ETHNE, a gentle Tuatha De Danann maiden, was lost to the otherworld when she mislaid her Veil of Invisibility, key to the Realm of Fairy. She was rescued by monks and, according to a later legend, became a nun, but she was disturbed by "voices", the cries of her fairy folk, seeking her in vain. (ILLUSTRATION BY STEPHEN REID, 1910.)

Fotla, went to greet them. All three asked that the newcomers would name the island after her. *AMAIRGEN*, druid and advisor to the sons of *MILESIUS*, promised that Ireland would be named after Eriu.

ETAIN, in Irish mythology, was one of the *TUATHA DE DANANN* and was reincarnated several times. She was the second wife of the god *MIDIR*. His first wife was jealous of Etain and by a druid's spell Etain was reborn as a mortal, the daughter of the Ulster warrior Etar. To hinder Midir's search for her, Etain was turned first into a pool of water, then a worm and finally a fly. When Etar's wife accidentally swallowed the fly she became pregnant with Etain. Unaware of her previous existence, Etain was loved both by the High King Eochaidh, whom she married, and by his brother *AILILL*. This potentially difficult situation was solved by her sudden discovery that she was already married to Midir, who had awakened her memories. High King Eochaidh lost Etain to the god at a game of chess, but although she lived once again with Midir for a period of time, Etain decided in the end to return to Tara and finish her mortal life as Eochaidh's queen.

ETHLINN, sometimes Ethnea, was the only daughter of *BALOR*, the one-eyed giant of Irish myth. Balor imprisoned Ethlinn in a crystal tower on Tory Island, off the north-western coast of Ireland, because of a prophecy that said he would be killed by his own grandson. However, a certain Cian, brother of the smith god *GOIBHNIU*, managed to reach Ethlinn, and so the sun god *LUGH* was conceived. Despite Balor's attempts to have the baby killed, he survived to be brought up either by Goibhniu or, according to another version of the myth, by the sea god *MANANNAN MAC LIR*, and so fulfilled his destiny by killing Balor at the second battle of Magh Tuireadh.

ETHNE was the daughter of Roc, steward of the love god *AONGHUS*, and acted as maid to the daughter of *MANANNAN MAC LIR*. After a chieftain of the *TUATHA DE DANANN* tried to rape her, she refused to eat or drink. Aonghus and Manannan searched for a remedy and found two magic cows whose milk never ran dry and she lived on their milk.

ETHNEA see *ETHLINN*

EXCALIBUR see *MAGIC AND ENCHANTMENT*

FAND, in Irish mythology, was the wife of *MANANNAN MAC LIR*. One day she quarrelled with her husband and he left her. When she was attacked by the *FOMORII*, Fand sent for *CUCHULAINN*, who came to her island and defeated her enemies, and remained for one month as her lover. Before he returned home, they arranged to meet again in Ireland. But Cuchulainn's wife, *EMER*, found out about this secret meeting and took fifty of her maidens armed with sharp knives to kill Fand. A confused argument then took place between Fand, Emer, Cuchulainn and Manannan Mac Lir, who had also learned of the arrangement. But in the end, Fand

FAND'S maidens appeared to Cuchulainn in a vision, beating him with rods, which left him sore for a year. Having gained his attention, they explained that the goddess, Fand, needed his help to fight the Fomorii. After defeating her attackers, Cuchulainn stayed on Fand's island for a month. (ILLUSTRATION BY STEPHEN REID, 1912.)

decided to stay with her husband and forget Cuchulainn. Manannan Mac Lir then shook his magic cloak between Fand and Cuchulainn so they would never see each other again, and druids gave Cuchulainn and Emer drinks of forgetfulness. (See also *CELTIC ROMANCE*)

FEDLIMID the story-teller was the father of *DEIRDRE*. One day, when *CONCHOBHAR MAC NESSA* and some fellow Ulstermen were drinking at his house, the unborn Deirdre cried out from her mother's womb. The druid *CATHBAD* then foretold that the child would cause nothing but doom and destruction.

FERDIA son of Daman the *FIRBOLG*, was a friend and comrade of *CUCHULAINN*. As young men, they were both taught to fight by *SCATHACH*. During the war of the brown bull of Cuailgne, Ferdia fought on the side of Queen *MEDB* and against Cuchulainn and the men of Ulster. Ferdia did his best to avoid coming up against his friend, but eventually Medb taunted him into fighting the great hero in single combat and he was killed.

FERGUS MAC LEDA see *MAGIC AND ENCHANTMENT*

FERGUS MAC ROTH, a king of Ulster, according to one myth fell in love with his predecessor's widow, *NESSA*. She would only marry him if her son, *CONCHOBHAR MAC NESSA*, was allowed to rule for a year. Conchobhar, with help from his mother, proved to be a popular king and the people refused to let him stand down. At first Fergus accepted this but, later, when Conchobhar lost the support of several leading Ulstermen, he led them in revolt. Conchobhar's love for *DEIRDRE* was the cause of his unpopularity, especially after he had her lover *NAOISE* killed in order to marry her. Fergus with three hundred Ulster warriors joined Queen *MEDB* in her invasion of Ulster. The great *CUCHULAINN* lost his life in this war, but not at the hands of Fergus. They had been friends before the war and had sworn not to fight each other. During the final battle, Fergus pretended to retreat and the next time they met Cuchulainn would do the same. It was due to Fergus' retreat that *CONALL*, Cuchulainn's foster-brother, was able to defeat Medb's army and rally the Ulstermen after the death of Cuchulainn.

FERDIA is borne from the battlefield by his lifelong friend, Cuchulainn. The two were goaded into single combat by Medb and fought grimly to the death. At Ferdia's death, Cuchulainn fell exhausted, lamenting, "Why should I rise again now he that lies here has fallen by my hand?" (ILLUSTRATION BY E WALLCOUSINS, 1912.)

THE FIANNA was the famous band of warriors responsible for the safety of the High King of Ireland. Popularly called the Fenians, their greatest leader was FINN MACCOOL and the majority of their members came from one of two clans, the Bascna and the Morna. Many of the adventures of the Knights of the Round Table recall the exploits of the Fenians. To join, "no man was taken till in the ground a hole had been made, such as would reach the waist, and he put into it with his shield and a forearm's length of a hazel stick. Then must nine warriors, having nine spears, with a ten furrows' width between them and him, assail him and let fly at him. If he sustained injury, he was not received into the band."

FINEGAS, in Irish mythology, was a druid. Hoping to become supremely wise, he caught the Salmon of Knowledge, but unfortunately for his own ambitions he gave it to the young FINN MACCOOL to cook. Finn burnt his thumb on the flesh of the fish and sucked the burn. Realizing that his pupil Finn was the one destined to gain the wisdom, Finegas generously let the boy eat the whole fish.

FINN MACCOOL, sometimes called Finn Mac Cumaill or Fionn MacCumal, was the leader of the FIANNA, or Fenians, the select band of warriors which guarded the High King of Ireland. His father, CUMAL, a previous leader of the Fenians, was killed by Goll, a Fenian warrior. Cumal had eloped with a girl named Hurna and her father urged Goll to avenge this dishonour. Goll slew Cumal, but later Cumal's son Finn was born and brought up secretly. One of his tutors was the druid FINEGAS, who lived beside the River Boyne and caught the Salmon of Knowledge. He gave the fish to his pupil to cook, but Finn burnt his thumb on the flesh and in sucking it obtained wisdom.

So great was Finn MacCool's prowess as a warrior that he was soon appointed over the head of Goll to lead the Fenians, as his father had done. Goll accepted this decision with good grace, a gesture that may explain why Finn MacCool did not challenge Goll over his father's death. Indeed, Goll eventually married one of Finn MacCool's daughters, though he also slew his son. This last act of violence was too much and the Fenians pursued him. Trapped, Goll chose to starve to death rather than surrender. Finn MacCool used to quote a saying of Goll: "A man lives after his life but not after his dishonour."

Under Finn MacCool's leadership, the Fenians reached the high point of their fame as a warrior band. The pursuit of DIARMUID UA DIUBHNE, the foster-son of the love god AONGHUS, alone took sixteen years. He had taken GRAINNE, the daughter of High King CORMAC MAC ART, but she was betrothed to Finn MacCool at the time. The Fenians were relentless in the chase, but a peace of sorts was begrudgingly agreed. However, Finn never forgave Diarmuid for

the elopement, and he exulted over his rival's mortal wound, which he had received when hunting.

The account of Finn MacCool's own death is unclear. Some sagas tell how he fell attempting to quell an uprising among the Fenians

THE FOMORII, *a misshapen race of sea gods, oppressed Ireland with cruelty and crushing tributes. This imaginative and powerful scene portrays the Fomorii as repellent and alien creatures, who are driven by a sick and menacing frenzy.*
(THE FOMORS OR THE POWERS OF EVIL ABROAD IN THE WORLD BY JOHN DUNCAN, 1912.)

themselves, while others refer to an *ARTHUR*-like undeath in a cave. There he was supposed to remain in a deep sleep until such time as Ireland needed his aid.

FINTAN was the husband of Noah's granddaughter *CESAIR*. It is likely that the monks who first recorded the Irish sagas altered the original myth in order to link it with Noah's descendants, because of the deluge that only Fintan managed to survive by becoming a salmon. The monks wanted to tidy up the Irish myth of Fintan's mysterious transformation. The same name was also given to the Salmon of Knowledge, which was so called because it had eaten the nuts of a hazel tree that grew over the waters of *NECHTAN*'s well.

THE FIRBOLG, or bag-men, arrived in Ireland after escaping a life of slavery in Thrace, where they had been forced to cultivate the land by heaving heavy bags of fertile earth up rocky hills. In revolt, they turned their bags into boats and sailed to Ireland. (ILLUSTRATION BY NICK BEALE, 1995.)

THE FIRBOLG, or "bag men", in Irish mythology were said to have acquired their name from a time when they were enslaved in Thrace and made to carry bags of earth. They lived in Ireland just before the arrival of the *TUATHA DE DANANN*. But they were already being hard pressed by the *FOMORII*, the sea gods whom the Tuatha De Danann eventually overcame. At the first battle of Magh Tuireadh the Tuatha De Danann defeated the Firbolg, though the De Danann leader, *NUADA*, lost a hand. In the second battle of Magh Tuireadh the Fomorii were thoroughly beaten, due mainly to the bravery of the sun god *LUGH*, and were driven from Ireland for ever.

THE FOMORII were sea gods in Irish mythology. Violent and misshapen, the Fomorii emerged from the waves to challenge two rulers of Ireland: the *FIRBOLG* and the *TUATHA DE DANANN*. The Tuatha De Danann were younger gods, and they seized control of Ireland from the Firbolgs at the first battle of Magh Tuireadh, only to have to defeat the Fomorii at a second battle there in order to secure their conquest. Often the Fomorii were described as having only a single hand, foot or eye.

FORBAI was the son of the Ulster king *CONCHOBHAR MAC NESSA*. According to one myth, Queen *MEDB* of Connacht fell back before the fury of the Ulster warriors after her invasion of the kingdom. In Galway, however, Forbai caught up with her as she was bathing in a lake. A shot from his sling fatally struck the old warrior-queen in the centre of her forehead.

FRAOCH ("wrath" or "fury"), in Irish mythology, was a warrior who defeated a fearsome water monster in order to marry Findbhair, who was the daughter of Queen *MEDB* of Connacht. The terrible struggle with the monster left Fraoch very badly wounded and he recovered fully only after a timely visit to the

otherworld. His mother Be Find (who was a goddess and sister of the river goddess *BOANN*) nursed him back to health so that he could claim the hand of Findbhair. The account of Fraoch and the water monster is thought to have had some influence on the Danish legend of Beowulf's battle with Grendel, a monster invulnerable to weapons who lived in an underwater cavern.

FINN MACCOOL stands guard on the ramparts of Tara awaiting a fiery goblin whose magic music usually disarms his foes. Armed with a fairy spear, Finn breaks the spell and slays the unsuspecting demon. For his valour he was made captain of the Fianna. (ILLUSTRATION BY STEPHEN REID, 1910.)

WONDROUS CAULDRONS

MIRACULOUS CAULDRONS feature as a recurrent motif in Celtic myth. Some overflow with plenty, others restore the dead to life, while still others contain a special brew of wisdom. Dagda's gigantic Cauldron of Plenty overflowed with abundant, delicious meats; no hero left his bowl hungry, though cowards never had their fill. From Bran's massive Cauldron of Rebirth warriors emerged alive but dumb; another Cauldron of Rebirth in Annwn was guarded by nine maidens. Cauldrons of Inspiration provided "greals" or brews of wisdom. The most famous belonged to the goddess Ceridwen, whose magical broth endowed Taliesin with all-knowing insight. Some cauldrons, such as Dagda's, combined the magical properties of both plenty and rebirth. Similar mystery bowls or cups feature in Greek and eastern myths as holy vessels of spiritual insight. Ultimately, the early Celtic cauldrons find expression in the Arthurian Grail, which overflows with spiritual sustenance and leads the hero from death to immortality.

CAULDRONS OF PLENTY (left) glittered in bronze, copper, silver or gold, embossed with exquisite craftsmanship. The gilded Gundestrup Cauldron, here, found in a bog in Denmark, is a magnificent surviving example of a Celtic cauldron. Embossed in silver gilt, it is beautifully decorated in the La Tene style with Celtic deities and ritual activities, such as hunting or fighting. (GUNDESTRUP CAULDRON, GILDED SILVER, 100 BC.)

BRAN'S (above) Cauldron of Rebirth restored warriors to life, but without the power of speech. Bran received his wondrous cauldron from two martial giants, in gratitude for his kindness. Here, the great and gloomy giants brood over their bubbling cauldron, flanked by armed warriors on either side, for the warlike giants produced a grown warrior every six weeks. (ILLUSTRATION BY ALAN LEE, 1984.)

THE GRAIL, *or Sangreal, (above) appeared to the knights of the Round Table amid dazzling light in which they saw each other more wisely and generously than ever before. The vision rendered them speechless, much like the Celtic warriors who emerged from their Cauldron of Rebirth alive but dumb. The Grail itself, shrouded in white samite, appears in the form of a Chalice of the Mass, recalling the Cup of the Last Supper. The chalice filled the hall with spicy odours and the knights ate and drank as never before, which all recalls the earlier Celtic Cauldrons of Plenty. (MANUSCRIPT ILLUSTRATION C. 1400.)*

CAULDRONS OF REBIRTH *(below), such as Annwn's or Bran's, must have been as large as tubs to contain the bodies of fallen warriors. In this section, a towering god appears to be dipping warriors into a mighty bucket or bowl, probably a cauldron of rebirth. Foot soldiers march in procession towards the cauldron, while a line of mounted infantry gallop off at the top, after their renovating dip. (CELTIC CAULDRON, GILDED SILVER, 100 BC.)*

CELTIC CAULDRONS *(below right) varied greatly in size, but such legendary cauldrons as Dagda's were so huge that they had to be conveyed on wheels or by chariot; while Bran's mighty cauldron was carried on the back of the giant Llaser. This cult wagon depicts just such a monumental cauldron. Mounted heroes in their peaked helmets, possibly hunters, travel triumphantly either to or from the hunt. The two stags, plus the hunters, suggest that the deity bearing the cauldron of plenty could well be the hunter god Cernunnos. (CULT WAGON, BRONZE, 100 BC.)*

G

GALAHAD (left), the pure and peerless knight, stands resplendent in a blaze of holy light, armed as a Christian Crusader. His snow-white shield, marked with the blood of Joseph of Arimathea, was designed in Sarras for Galahad alone. (GALAHAD BY W HATHERELL, GLASS, C. 1910.)

GALAHAD (right), robed in red, entered Arthur's court escorted by a hermit, and took his place at the Round Table, filling the Siege Perilous. Completing the circle of knights, his arrival sparked off the Grail Quest. (GALAHAD ENTERS ARTHUR'S COURT BY W HATHERELL, CANVAS, C. 1910.)

GALAHAD was unique at the court of King *ARTHUR*, for he alone saw the entire Grail, or *SANGREAL*. He may even have handled the sacred vessel, as one version of the Arthurian myth states that Sir Galahad took "Our Lord's body between his hands" and then died. The quest for the Grail was an important preoccupation of the Knights of the Round Table. One of the seats was always left vacant as it was the place reserved for the knight who would find the Grail. Until Sir Galahad sat there, no knight had earned the right to occupy the place without being instantly swallowed by the earth.

The worthy young Sir Galahad was the son of Sir *LANCELOT*, the secret lover of Queen *GUINEVERE*, Arthur's wife. From the beginning of Galahad's manhood, however, it is made clear that he is without blemish. Twelve nuns, who had raised Galahad, told his father that he should "make him a knight, for there is no man alive more deserving of the order of knighthood". As soon as Sir Galahad had taken his rightful place at the Round Table, the presence of the Grail was felt in

GALAHAD receives spiritual nourishment from the Grail, followed by Percival and Bors. The idea of an all-sustaining and all-inspiring "greal" or brew is rooted in Celtic myth. (HOW SIR GALAHAD, SIR BORS AND SIR PERCIVAL WERE FED WITH THE SANC GREAL BY DANTE ROSSETTI, CANVAS, 1864.)

Camelot. A mysterious lady then announced how the sacred vessel would come and feed all the knights. This happened, although none at the wonderful meal saw or touched the Grail. When Sir Gawain vowed to find its home in order to see the Grail for himself, most of the Knights of the Round Table followed suit, despite the efforts of King Arthur to dissuade them from undertaking what might prove to be their final quest. Although they set off in different directions, Sir Galahad was in the company of Sir *PERCIVAL* and Sir Bors when he encountered the Grail. Together they had received the sacrament from the long-dead *JOSEPH OF ARIMATHEA*, who told Sir Galahad to take a bleeding spear to the castle of the "Maimed King" and rub it on this crippled ruler's body and limbs. Once this task was carried out, and the strange king restored to health, Sir Galahad saw the Grail in a vision. When he prayed that "he might leave the world", a voice told him how his soul would live in the next life with Christ the moment his request could be granted.

After this, various miracles took place and Sir Galahad was even obliged to become a king for a time while he waited patiently for his request to be fulfilled. When Joseph of Arimathea eventually returned, Galahad was at last granted his wish to leave the world. Joseph first allowed the pure and humble knight to hold the Grail for a few moments, then, as Sir Galahad knelt down to pray for his deliverance, his soul was suddenly released from his body and "a great multitude of angels bore it up to heaven".

GAWAIN, in Welsh Gwalchmai, was the most courteous knight at *ARTHUR*'s court. He was a strict upholder of chivalry and the enemy of Sir *LANCELOT*. Sir Gawain's most extraordinary adventure concerned the Green Knight. Rather like the hazard faced by the Ulster hero *CUCHULAINN*, when a water giant came to test the courage of Irish warriors, the gigantic Green Knight strode into King Arthur's hall at Camelot one New Year's Eve and challenged the Knights of the Round Table to a beheading contest. Sir Gawain accepted and cut off the stranger's head in a single blow. As the severed head rolled around the hall, the royal court relaxed and thought the challenge over. But to the amazement of all

present, the giant behaved as if nothing had happened. Calmly stooping, he picked up his head and mounted his green charger. Then, from the saddle, the Green Knight pointed his severed head in Sir Gawain's direction and told him to be at a lonely chapel a year from that day in order to take a turn at receiving a blow from an axe. On the journey to this dangerous appointment Sir Gawain stayed with Sir Bercilak de Hautdesert who had a beautiful wife. He was sorely tempted by Sir Bercilak's wife but managed to resist her advances for two days. However, on the third day Sir Gawain accepted from her a green sash, which was the usual token worn by a knight to show his love for a lady.

At the meeting between Sir Gawain and his fearful opponent, the Green Knight turned out to be none other than Sir Bercilak himself. Three times the axe was swung at Sir Gawain's neck. Twice it was deflected because he had not abused his host's hospitality by making love to his wife. The third time it made a slight cut, at which Sir Gawain flinched. It did not cut off his head because Sir Gawain had only accepted the green sash out of good manners. Yet Sir Gawain realized that courtesy was no equal to moral purity, and thereafter he always wore the green sash as a reminder of his lapse.

This late British version of the Celtic beheading contest was quite clearly influenced by Christianity.

GAWAIN, an active and restless knight, lost interest in the Grail Quest quite early on. Although one of the first to set forth, inspiring the rest of the Knights, he lost heart, lacking the necessary discipline, patience and humility. (THE FAILURE OF SIR GAWAIN BY W MORRIS, TAPESTRY, 1895–96.)

Unlike Sir Gawain, Cuchulainn had no hesitation in slipping away from the battlefield in order to keep a secret meeting with a lover, even during Queen *MEDB*'s invasion of Ulster. The magical transformation of Sir Bercilak de Hautdesert into the Green Knight was explained as the work of the witch *MORGAN LE FAY*, King Arthur's half-sister.

GERAINT see *CELTIC ROMANCE; SINGLE COMBAT*

H

GOIBHNIU was the Irish smith god and one of the *TUATHA DE DANANN*. He could make a perfect sword or spear with three blows of his magic hammer. Just before the second battle of Magh Tuireadh, a *FOMORII* spy came to see how Goibhniu made such impressive weapons, and even wounded the god. Goibhniu was said to preside over an otherworld feast called *Fled Goibnenn*, for which he brewed the ale. His Welsh counterpart was named Govannon.

THE GRAIL see *SANGREAL*; see also *WONDROUS CAULDRONS*; *HEROIC QUESTS*.

GRAINNE, in Irish mythology, was the daughter of *CORMAC MAC ART*, the High King of Ireland. She was promised to *FINN MACCOOL*, leader of the *FIANNA*, the bodyguard of the High King. Although still powerful, Finn MacCool was quite old and Grainne preferred *DIARMUID UA DUIBHNE*, who was

GOIBHNIU, the Irish smith god, was an outstanding craftsman and armourer. Along with his gifted brothers, Creidhne the goldsmith, and Luchtar, the carpenter, he repaired the Tuatha De Danann armour with miraculous speed on the battlefield. (ILLUSTRATION ANON.)

the foster-son of the love god *AONGHUS*. By using magic, Grainne managed to escape from Tara, the Irish capital, with a rather reluctant Diarmuid. Gradually, however, he came to love Grainne, although for sixteen years they had to keep moving in order to avoid capture

by the Fenians. But Diarmuid was killed by a magic boar in a hunting accident after Cormac Mac Art and Finn MacCool had finally accepted his marriage to Grainne. Although Grainne blamed Finn MacCool for Diarmuid's death and swore to obtain vengeance through her four sons, the wily Finn wooed her until she agreed to marry him.

GUINEVERE, whose Welsh name, Gwenhwyfar, probably means "white spirit", was the wife of *ARTHUR* and the secret lover of Sir *LANCELOT*. In the stories about the Knights of the Round Table, Guinevere is always compared with Helen of Troy, the famous beauty of Greek mythology. Such a comparison is not unjustified, for both these women brought disaster to those who loved them. In Guinevere's case the love affair with Sir Lancelot weakened the unity of the Round Table. It was her beauty that also attracted Arthur's nephew Sir *MODRED*, who seized Camelot

GRAINNE (above), a passionate and wilful maiden, fell for the irresistible Diarmuid. As she was betrothed to Finn MacCool, Diarmuid politely refused her advances. But she persisted until he agreed to elope, with the Fianna in hot pursuit. Here, the guilty pair hide in a magic tree. (ILLUSTRATION ANON.)

GUINEVERE (below), in her original role as Flower Bride, is crowned May Queen in a bower of petals. On May Morning, Arthur and his knights celebrated with sports and contests. Lancelot, her champion, always excelled. (LANCELOT AND GUINEVERE BY HERBERT DRAPER, CANVAS, 1900.)

GUINEVERE (above), condemned to death for her affair with Lancelot, was rescued by him. In the bloody contest that ensued, Lancelot slew many knights. Arthur wept at the loss of "the fairest fellowship of noble knights". (LANCELOT RESCUES GUINEVERE BY W HATHERELL, CANVAS, C. 1910.)

and forced Guinevere to consent to marry him during the king's absence abroad. The confrontation between Arthur and Modred at the battle of Camlan brought to a bloody end the golden age of British chivalry, as hardly a knight was left alive. Arthur, mortally wounded, was taken to *AVALON*, while Guinevere became a nun at Amesbury, where she later died. It is believed by some that her body was buried at Glastonbury, not far from Arthur's tomb. (See also *CELTIC ROMANCE*)

GWERN, according to Welsh mythology, was the son of the Irish king *MATHOLWCH* and the Welsh princess *BRANWEN*. A dispute between the two royal families led to Branwen becoming a cook, which caused her brother, *BRAN THE BLESSED*, to sail to Ireland to avenge the insult. Matholwch suggested a compromise to settle the

quarrel. He proposed that Gwern, though only three, should be placed on the Irish throne. But Branwen's half-brother *EFNISIEN* would not agree and threw the child on to a fire.

GWYDION was the nephew of *MATH*, lord of the Welsh kingdom of Gwynedd. In order to help his brother, Gilvaethwy, sleep with Gowein, the young woman who was Math's footholder, Gwydion stirred up a quarrel between Math and *PRYDERI*, which meant that the king went away to war. When Math returned and discovered the deception, he turned his nephews into a stag and a hind for one year, into a boar and a sow for the next, and into a pair of wolves for the third. Later, Gwydion took charge of his sister *ARIANRHOD*'s son *LLEU*.

GWION BACH see *TALIESIN*.

GWYN AP NUDD, in Welsh mythology, was an otherworld king who crossed swords with King *ARTHUR*. Gwyn abducted Griddylad, the daughter of Lludd Llaw Ereint, on her wedding day. According to one late myth, Lludd Llaw Ereint was the son of the death god Beli

and the builder of London. King Arthur set out after Griddylad and demanded that Gwyn ap Nudd return her to her rightful husband, his loyal follower Gwythyr. The siege of the otherworld king's castle proved to be long and difficult, so a strange compromise was agreed by both sides. Gwyn ap Nudd and Gwythyr agreed to meet in combat each May Day until the end of time; whoever was the winner on doomsday could have Griddylad.

HELLAWES see *SAGES AND SEERS*.

IRNAN, in Irish mythology, was a witch who once spun a magic web to catch some members of the *FIANNA*, or Fenians, the bodyguard of the High King of Ireland. When this plan failed, Irnan changed herself into a monster and challenged any one of the Fenians to single combat. *FINN MACCOOL*, the leader of the Fenians, stepped forward but was persuaded that it would not be heroic enough for a warrior of his stature to fight a hag, even if she was in the form of a monster. So another Fenian, Goll, slew Irnan and as a reward Finn allowed him to marry his daughter.

GWYDION (above) and Gilvaethwy flee from Pryderi's castle with his precious swine. The daring theft was part of an ingenious plan to help Gilvaethwy win Gowein. A resourceful magician, Gwydion had tricked Pryderi into exchanging his swine for some illusory horses. (ILLUSTRATION BY ALAN LEE, 1984.)

IRNAN (below) was one of three sister witches. She spun a magic web to snare the Fenian warriors. The warriors were rescued by Goll who slew two of the sisters, but spared Irnan when she begged for mercy. However, Irnan instantly changed into a monster and Goll killed her. (ILLUSTRATION BY STEPHEN REID, 1910.)

ISEULT, sometimes Isolde, was an Irish princess, and the story of her love for *TRISTAN* was extremely popular in medieval times. The Celtic myth of Tristan and Iseult originated in Brittany and was retold in almost every European country. It became attached to the Arthurian stories by the later addition of *ARTHUR* to the myth.

Iseult, a beautiful woman with wonderful golden hair, cured the orphan Tristan of a wound in the side; a lingering ailment similar to the one afflicting the "Maimed King" in the story of the Grail. On Tristan's arrival in Cornwall, his uncle King *MARK* wanted to name the young man his successor, but the nobles objected to this arrangement, so the king said that he would marry only the girl to whom belonged the golden hair a swallow had just dropped. Sir Tristan, recognizing the hair as belonging to Iseult, suggested to his uncle that he should go on his behalf to ask for her hand.

Disguised as a Cornish trader, Sir Tristan arrived in Ireland to find the country terrorized by a dragon,

ISEULT (below), an Irish beauty, was also a gifted healer, and cured the Cornish knight Tristan of a lingering wound. While nursing him to health, they fell in love, but their bliss was shortlived as Tristan was forced to leave the Irish court for political reasons. (ILLUSTRATION BY EVELYN PAUL, C. 1900.)

an enormous "crested serpent". Realizing that the best way to advance King Mark's suit would be to slay this monster, Sir Tristan sought out its lair and fought it. Although he just managed to overcome the dragon, its poisonous breath weakened him temporarily and an imposter claimed to have won the contest. Iseult and her mother, however, suspected trickery and discovered the injured young knight. While they were nursing Sir Tristan back to health, Iseult noticed that his sword had a piece missing exactly like the fragment of metal found in the head of *MORHOLT*, the Irish champion. Sir Tristan had mortally wounded him on the last occasion the Irish tried to collect tribute from Cornwall.

Iseult wanted to kill Sir Tristan in revenge, but she found that her heart would not let her wield the sword against him. It came as a

shock then, on his recovery, that Sir Tristan asked for Iseult on behalf of King Mark. When her own father readily agreed to the marriage as a means of restoring good relations between Ireland and Cornwall, Iseult was deeply upset. But her mother gave Iseult's maid *BRANGAINE* a love potion which, if drunk on their wedding night, would make the couple love each other forever. All would have been well had not Tristan accidentally drunk the potion and given some to Iseult on the journey to King Mark's court. Although Iseult did marry the Cornish king, on the wedding night, under the cover of darkness, Brangaine took her place in the royal bed so that he would suspect nothing. For a time the lovers managed to meet in secret, but, like the love of *GUINEVERE* and *LANCELOT*, they were eventually discovered. It happened one day

ISEULT and Tristan unwittingly drank a love philtre which heightened their already awakened passion, forging an unbreakable and finally tragic bond. Duncan's strongly Celtic portrayal captures the intense and undying nature of their love. (TRISTAN AND ISOLDE BY JOHN DUNCAN, CANVAS, 1912.)

that King Mark found them asleep with Sir Tristan's sword between them, but he decided not to slay them there and then. Instead he exchanged Sir Tristan's sword for his own and left them sleeping. Overcome by the mercy shown by his uncle, Tristan persuaded Iseult to return to her husband and he left for voluntary exile in Brittany.

In Brittany Sir Tristan married but without happiness. On several occasions he returned to Cornwall in disguise and secretly met Iseult again, but war took up most of his energies. A serious wound forced Sir Tristan to send for Iseult. It was agreed that Iseult should indicate her imminent arrival with a white sail. Jealous of the reunion of the lovers, Sir Tristan's Breton wife said a ship with a black sail had been sighted. Tristan lost the will to live and threw himself on his sword before Iseult could land and reach his bedside. Iseult followed him into death shortly afterwards.

Stories of elopements, courtships and ill-fated lovers were always popular with the Celts, for whom this late story of frustrated passion held great appeal. (See also CELTIC ROMANCE)

ITH was said to have dwelt in a great tower in Spain, from which he was able to see Ireland and so decided to go there. He landed with ninety followers just after the TUATHA DE DANANN had defeated the FOMORII at the second battle of Magh Tuireadh. The Tuatha De Danann suspected Ith of harbouring invasion plans and so killed him. When his body was returned to Spain, his sons swore to conquer the island. The leader of this

IUBDAN (below), one of the Wee Folk, was inclined to brag of his greatness, inciting his bard to cut him down to size by insisting that far greater men lived in Ulster, a veritable race of giants. To prove his valour, Iubdan ventured off to the dun of the "giant", Fergus Mac Leda. (ILLUSTRATION BY STEPHEN REID, 1910.)

invasion of Ireland, the last to be recorded in Irish mythology, was Ith's uncle Mil, or MILESIUS.

IUBDAN was a ruler of tiny people. According to Irish mythology, King Iubdan liked to boast a lot; to put a stop to this annoying habit his court poet told him that Ulster was a land of giants. He even made King Iubdan and his wife, Queen Bebo, travel there in secret and try the porridge of the king of Ulster, Fergus Mac Leda. Unfortunately, Iubdan fell into the porridge and, along with his wife, was taken prisoner by Fergus. No ransom offer proved acceptable to the king of Ulster, although the tiny people offered him an abundant crop of corn. So they went on to the offensive: milk became scarce, rivers and wells were made foul and polluted, mills burned and during the nights the hair of

JOSEPH OF ARIMATHEA (above), the man who interred Christ's body in his own tomb, is believed to have brought the Grail to Glastonbury. After building a church for it where Glastonbury Abbey now stands, he founded a family of Grail Guardians. (MANUSCRIPT ILLUSTRATION C. 1450.)

men and women was entirely cut off. After a year and a day of this harassment Fergus Mac Leda eventually agreed to release Iubdan and Bebo, but only on the condition that in return he was given the king's most valuable and treasured possession, a pair of magic shoes. Whoever wore these shoes was able to travel across the surface of water as if walking on dry land, and when Fergus Mac Leda put them on they grew to fit his feet exactly. Echoes of the tiny people in this Irish myth can be found in Jonathan Swift's novel, *Gulliver's Travels*.

KAI (above), Arthur's steward, was a knight of legendary might and prowess. Endowed with unusual skills, he could go for nine days underwater and could grow as tall as a forest tree at will. He was very gruff, thwarting both Peredur and Culhwch at the gate. (MANUSCRIPT ILLUSTRATION C. 1450.)

JOSEPH OF ARIMATHEA was a biblical figure who was included in Arthurian mythology because of the Grail story. Joseph allowed Christ's body to be placed in his own tomb. His own long life was said to have been due to the Grail. Either Joseph, or his brother-in-law Bron with his son Alan, brought the Grail to Glastonbury. Later, it disappeared and its recovery was the greatest quest for the Knights of the Round Table. Only GALAHAD was granted a complete vision of the Grail. It was handed to him by Joseph of Arimathea, a "bishop already dead for more than three hundred years"; this "good man took Our Lord's body between his hands, and offered it to Sir Galahad, who received it with humble joy".

KAI, in Welsh mythology, was one of the senior warriors of ARTHUR's court. In medieval romance, he became the steward Sir Kay. In one tradition, he is a Cornishman and Arthur's foster-brother. He was said to have magical powers: he could go nine days and nine nights without sleep and breathe for nine days and nine nights under water.

KAY see KAI

CELTIC ROMANCE

THE LIVELY AND COMPELLING character of Celtic romance stems from the theated rivalries and passions of the lovers. Most, if not all, tales involve a love triangle with two men contesting one desirable woman. Sometimes one of the rivals is young and handsome, while the other is an oppressive guardian, as in the tale of Naoise and Conchobhar; elsewhere, the two suitors are simply rival admirers, one loved and the other despised, as in the case of Pwyll and Gwawl. This recurrent rivalry probably symbolizes a seasonal battle between a Lord of Summer and a Lord of Winter for the Spring Maiden. Celtic love triangles create tension, drama and colourful characters of timeless appeal. The attractive young heroes, such as raven-haired Naoise, or Diarmuid of the Love-Spot, are quite as irresistible as the ravishing Celtic beauties, Deirdre and Fand. While all the characters are portrayed with touching flaws, the heroines emerge as strong and independent women, expressing warmth and wisdom.

LANCELOT (above) and Guinevere's abiding love for each other wounded Arthur, shook his court and split the Fellowship of Knights. Yet both lovers are portrayed by Mallory as essentially good but tragic characters. Even Arthur realized that Guinevere had been true to him in her way as a generous and faithful consort, and he was never lessened by their love. Here, the couple kiss at their first meeting, contrived by Galleot in an embroidered medieval setting. Although their love grew out of the courtly tradition, it went far beyond what the courtly code would have allowed. (MANUSCRIPT ILLUSTRATION C. 1400.)

TRISTAN (above) and Iseult snatch a tense moment together in their clandestine romance. They had grown obsessively attached to one another after accidentally drinking a love philtre intended for Iseult and her betrothed, King Mark of Cornwall. The doomed lovers embarked on a desperate and tragic romance, fraught with guilt and unrequited longings. (TRISTAN AND ISOLDE BY A W TURNBALL, CANVAS, 1904.)

THE LADY OF THE FOUNTAIN (right), a shining vision in gold, appeared to young Owain as the fairest, wisest, noblest, most chaste, most generous woman in the world. But, as Owain had just slain her husband, the Black Knight, he had to press his suit with care. The Lady's faithful handmaiden, Luned, helped Owain woo her mistress by reminding her that the realm required a strong guardian. Luned here escorts Owain to her Lady's chamber. (ILLUSTRATION BY ALAN LEE, 1984.)

FAND (above), a breathtaking beauty from the otherworld, set her heart on the Ulster hero, Cuchulainn, and lured him to her realm to fight a Fomorii giant. After a month in her delightful company, the two arranged a tryst where the hero's wife, Emer, joined them, lamenting, "What's new is sweet, what's well-known is sour…" Her heartfelt plea inspired the generous Fand to give up her beloved Cuchulainn, realizing that he had a worthy mate in Emer. (ETAIN, HELEN, MAEV AND FAND BY HARRY CLARKE, GLASS, DETAIL, C. 1900.)

GERAINT (right), suspecting his wife of infidelity, forced her to accompany him on a gruelling journey of errands, and so tested her love and obedience every step of the way. Like other strong-minded Celtic heroines, Enid endured her ordeal calmly, remaining loyal and loving throughout. Geraint, for his part, finally felt "two sorrows" of remorse for having mistrusted and mistreated her so. At one stage in their journey, the pair passed through a wonderful walled tower, as seen here.

(ILLUSTRATION BY ALAN LEE, 1984.)

L

LAEG was *CUCHULAINN*'s charioteer. The Celts were renowned in the ancient world for their skill in handling chariots on the battlefield, and Laeg's skill was crucial to many of Cuchulainn's victories. He was also a great friend and companion. When *FAND* invited Cuchulainn to the Land of Promise, he sent Laeg before him to survey the place. During Cuchulainn's final and mortal combat, Laeg threw himself in front of a spear aimed at his master. Id, Laeg's brother, was charioteer to *CONALL* Caernach.

LAEG, charioteer of Cuchulainn, drove the hero on all his adventures, acted as scout and comrade and finally cast himself in front of a spear meant for his master. War chariots played a key role in Celtic battle, with driver and warrior acting as a single unit. (ILLUSTRATION BY J LEYENDECKER, 1916.)

LANCELOT, most handsome and gifted of Arthur's knights, attracted both mortal and immortal queens. Four fairy queens here kidnap the sleeping knight and hold him in their castle, demanding that he choose one of them to be his mistress. (HOW FOUR FAIRY QUEENS FOUND LANCELOT SLEEPING BY W F CALDERON, CANVAS, C. 1900.)

LANCELOT was one of the greatest and noblest knights in the Arthurian tales. He was known as Lancelot of the Lake because the Lady of the Lake had plunged him into a magic pool when he was a child. Sir Lancelot, described as "the flower of knights", was very attractive to women, not unlike the handsome Irish warrior *DIARMUID UA DUIBHNE*. Once King *ARTHUR*'s half-sister and enemy *MORGAN LE FAY* cast a spell over the sleeping knight and shut him in a dungeon. There she demanded that he must choose among four enchantresses who would be his "paramour", or mistress. When he turned them all down, including Morgan Le Fay, the knight admitted his love for *GUINEVERE*. All of Sir Lancelot's great adventures and exploits were indeed informed by this secret love. For a time Queen Guinevere would not allow Sir Lancelot to come to her, but they eventually became lovers. Sir Meliagaunt, however, was suspicious and confronted Sir Lancelot in the presence of King Arthur and Queen Guinevere. A tournament was held to discover the truth. "With such great force Sir Lancelot smote Sir Meliagaunt on the helmet that the stroke carved the head into two parts."

LANCELOT, after much fasting and praying, came at last to Carbonek, the Grail Castle. Being tainted with sin, he could not enter but was granted a vision. When he stepped too close he was struck by fire and left dazed for 24 days. (LANCELOT REFUSED THE GRAIL BY E BURNE-JONES, CANVAS, 1870.)

Honour seemed satisfied and the reputation of Arthur's queen also appeared unblemished, but there were other Knights of the Round Table who could not accept this judgement by arms. So Sir Agravain and Sir *MODRED* led twelve knights to Guinevere's chamber and surprised the lovers. Although Sir Lancelot managed to make a fighting exit and several days later saved Queen Guinevere from being burnt to death, his actions effectively split the Round Table and weakened the strength of King Arthur's realm. First, Arthur conducted an unsuccessful siege of Sir Lancelot's castle in Brittany. Then a second and more deadly challenge to the king's authority came from Sir Modred, his nephew. In the subsequent battle at Camlan, near Salisbury, most of the Knights of the Round Table were slain. King Arthur was mortally wounded and taken by a magic boat to *AVALON*. Queen Guinevere retreated from the world and became a nun at Amesbury, where she died. Sir Lancelot and Guinevere met only once more before the knight renounced the ways of war to lead the life of a hermit. (See also *CELTIC ROMANCE*)

LLEU (right) had to turn into an eagle to escape his murderous wife, Blodeuedd. He hid in the forest, wounded and starving, until Gwydion lured him down and restored him to health. Blodeuedd was turned into an owl. (ILLUSTRATION BY ALAN LEE, 1984.)

LIR, or Llyr in Welsh, was the father of *MANANNAN MAC LIR*, the Manx sea god, magician and god of healing. Although Lir was also a sea god he is hardly mentioned in mythology, despite giving his name to many places, including Leicester in England. Shakespeare probably had the Welsh Llyr in mind when he wrote his tragedy *King Lear*.

LLEU, named Lleu of the Skilful Hand, in Welsh mythology was the son of *ARIANRHOD*. His mother laid a series of curses upon him, including the promise that he was to have no name unless she gave him one, no weapons unless she provided them and no wife of the human race. With the help of his uncle *GWYDION*, who raised him, Lleu overcame all these taboos, though the wife conjured by Gwydion and the magician *MATH* was nearly his undoing. For this woman, *BLODEUEDD*, fell in love with

LIR'S four lovely children were turned into swans by their jealous stepmother. For 900 years they endured cold and hunger in icy waters, charming listeners with their poignant song. When at last restored to human form, they were bent and bony. (LIR'S CHILDREN BY JOHN DUNCAN, CANVAS, 1912.)

another man and plotted Lleu's death. When the guilty lovers struck him, Lleu rose into the air in the shape of an eagle. After a long search, Gwydion found him, restored him to human form and healed his wounds.

LLUD see *NUDD*

LUGH was the Irish name for the Celtic sun god, who was known as Lleu in Wales and as Lugos in France. He was always described as a young and handsome warrior.

Lugh was himself part *FOMORII*, since his grandfather was the Irish one-eyed god *BALOR*, the Fomorii champion. The Fomorii were sea gods who challenged the *TUATHA DE DANANN* for control of Ireland; they were sometimes described as having only a single hand, foot or eye. Lugh's mother was *ETHLINN*, the only daughter of Balor. Because a prophecy had said that Balor would be killed by his own grandson, he locked Ethlinn in a crystal tower on Tory Island, off the northwestern coast of Ireland. But Cian, son of the Tuatha De Danann healing god *DIAN CECHT*, succeeded in reaching Ethlinn and she bore Lugh as a result. Either the sea god *MANANNAN MAC LIR* or the smith

god *GOIBHNIU*, Cian's brother, saved Lugh from Balor's wrath and raised him to manhood.

Well before the final battle between the Tuatha De Danann and the Fomorii, Lugh's prowess as a warrior had been recognized. The De Danann leader *NUADA* stepped down in his favour, and at the second battle of Magh Tuireadh Lugh fulfilled the prophecy of Balor's death when he killed him with a sling-shot. Before delivering this decisive blow Lugh had circled the enemy host on one foot and with one eye closed, a magic circuit that copied the single-leggedness of the Fomorii in general and one-eyed Balor in particular. It would seem that, like the Ulster hero *CUCHULAINN* and the berserkers of Germanic mythology, the battle-frenzy gripped Lugh in such a way that one eye disappeared into his head while the other expanded into a hideous, paralysing stare. Balor's own single eyelid had to be raised by four servants, and Lugh sent his shot smashing into the eye the moment it was opened. Balor's eye was forced back through his head, with the result that its terrible gaze fell upon the Fomorii ranks behind. Thus Balor died and the Fomorii scattered. Lugh became known as

Lamfhada ("of the Long Arm") Quite possibly this great victory represented the rise of younger gods amongst the Tuatha De Danann themselves, for the youthful Lugh felled Balor with a more modern weapon than *DAGDA*'s ancient club. Indeed, an alternative name for Lugh was Samildanach ("the many-skilled"). This ingenuity may account for Lugh's introduction as the father of Cuchulainn in the more historical sagas. The sun god was believed to have fought alongside his hard-pressed son during Queen *MEDB* of Connacht's invasion of Ulster. After Cuchulainn's death his foster-brother *CONALL* claimed to have received help from Lugh when he chased Cuchulainn's killers. On one occasion the sun god appeared in a magic mist.

Lugh's final claim to fame is that his name became part of the term used to describe the fairy in Irish folklore, because over time "Little stooping Lugh", or Luchorpain, turned into the leprechaun, the tiny guardian of hidden treasure and the expert cobbler.

LUGH, the resplendent Celtic sun god, led the Tuatha De Danann against the Fomorii led by his grandfather, Balor, whom he slew with his magic sling-shot. As god of arts and crafts, he invented the popular board game of fidchell, in which he excelled. (ILLUSTRATION BY E WALLCOUSINS, 1912.)

LUGUS was the name used in Britain and France for a god very similar to the Irish *LUGH* and the Welsh *LLEU*. His importance can be judged from the old name for Lyon, Lugdunum ("the fortress of Lug"). The Roman emperor Augustus made it the capital of the provinces of Gaul, and ordered the inhabitants to celebrate this choice each August, the month in which the feast of the Celtic sun god Lugus occurred. The god's name was used for many other place names, possibly even London: the Roman Londinium may have derived from Lugdunum.

MABON, son of the Welsh divine mother Modron, was said to have been abducted when only three nights old and imprisoned in Gloucester. However, since only he was able to control the hound which *CULHWCH* needed to win the hand of *OLWEN*, an expedition was mounted to release Mabon. Once free, he duly helped to capture the wild boar *TWRCH TRWYTH* with the aid of the hound and to take from between the boar's ears the razor

MACHA cursed the Ulstermen to suffer the pain of childbirth for five days, at the time of Ulster's greatest need. The bitter curse stemmed from her ill-treatment by the Ulstermen when, though near her term, she was forced to race on foot to prove a bet. (ILLUSTRATION BY STEPHEN REID, 1910.)

that Olwen's father had demanded. Apart from adventures like this, the actions of Mabon are uncertain, suggesting that he may have been a former god, possibly Maponos, a Celtic god of youth, who was incorporated in Welsh mythology as a warrior once his worship was all but forgotten. The Romans knew of Maponos, whom they equated with Apollo, the god of prophecy.

MAC CECHT was the Irish god of eloquence and the son of *OGMA*. After *NUADA* had been killed at the second battle of Magh Tuireadh, Mac Cecht and his brothers could not decide whether to divide Ireland between them and so they consulted a stranger named *ITH*. Suspecting from his response that he had designs on conquering the island himself, they killed him, thus provoking the invasion of the sons of *MILESIUS*.

MAC DA THO was king of Leinster at the time that *MEDB* was queen of Connacht. He owned a fine hound and a huge boar, and many of his neighbours coveted these animals, including Medb and *CONCHOBHAR MAC NESSA*, king of

MABON, or Maponos, was the youthful Welsh love god. A gifted musician, he was also equated with the classical god Apollo. Although forgotten as a god, Maponos survived in Welsh myth as Mabon, a skilled hunter among Arthur's champions. (ILLUSTRATION BY MIRANDA GRAY, 1994.)

Ulster. Mac Da Tho promised both these rulers that they could have the hound, and slaughtered the boar to provide a feast, to which he invited them. Fighting broke out between the Ulster king and the men of Connacht, but the latter soon retreated. When the hound, over which they had been quarrelling, ran after the king's chariot his charioteer cut off its head.

MACHA was one of the Irish war goddesses, often identified with *BADB*, *MORRIGAN* and *NEMAIN*. She first married Nemed, a Scythian ruler who defeated the *FOMORII*, the sea gods who slew her second husband *NUADA* and herself at the second battle of Magh Tuireadh. A later Macha laid a curse on Ulster after her boastful husband said that, though heavy with child, she could outrun all the king's horses and chariots. When the king of

Ulster threatened to execute her husband if she did not race, Macha cursed all Ulstermen to suffer the pain of childbirth for five days and five nights whenever the kingdom was in danger. Macha won the race and gave birth to twins, which is said to be the reason for calling the fortress of the Ulster kings Emain Macha ("Macha's Twins").

MAELDUN, or Mael Duin, was one of the great Irish voyagers. The late saga that describes his voyage is a mixture of Christian and pre-Christian ideas, in contrast to the fundamentally pre-Christian mythical voyage of the earlier *BRAN*.

Maeldun's father was a chieftain of the Aran Islands who attacked the Irish mainland, looted a church and raped a nun. He was killed shortly afterwards by raiders from overseas, in all likelihood Vikings. The nun gave birth to Maeldun and the child was fostered by the local ruler's wife, who was the sister of the unfortunate nun. It was only when children taunted Maeldun that he was not really well born that his foster-mother took him to see his true mother and his parentage was revealed. He then set out with three of his foster-brothers to find his father, only to learn that he had been murdered.

Determined to avenge his father's death, Maeldun was advised by a druid as to which were the favourable days for him to build, launch and sail a three-skinned coracle. Then, still accompanied by his foster-brothers and also a crew of seventeen warriors, he sailed on his long and strange voyage of revenge.

The first island Maeldun came to was inhabited by murderers, but apparently not the killers of his father. Next they landed upon an isle of enormous ants; as large as horses, the ants almost devoured the crew and the boat. Large birds living on another island were found to pose no threat, however. They even provided the voyagers with

on top of a pedestal; the offer of eternal youth on one island which was inhabited by a queen and her daughters; intoxicating fruits; contagious laughter; revolving fire; and a hermit who lived on salmon that was given by an otter and half a loaf provided each day by angels.

Eventually, Maeldun caught up with his father's killers, but they pleaded for mercy and a peace was agreed. Thus ended the voyage that was said to contain "the sum of the wisdom of Ireland". (See also *FABULOUS VOYAGES*)

MAEVE see *MEDB*.

MAELDUN (below) and his sailors found a wondrous silver column rising straight from the sea. Its summit, lost in the sky, was draped with a silver net, flung far out to sea. As they sailed through the mesh, Diurnan hacked off a piece as proof of the tale. (ILLUSTRATION BY DANUTA MEYER, 1994.)

MAELDUN, on his epic voyage, stopped by the bleak island of the mill (above) where lived a gloomy miller grimly grinding mounds of corn. He observed dourly that the corn symbolized all that men begrudged each other. The voyagers, aghast, sailed away. (ILLUSTRATION BY ALAN LEE, 1984.)

meat. Two subsequent islands of monstrous, gigantic horses proved to be even more dangerous, so it was with some relief that Maeldun and his companions landed on the Island of the House of the Salmon. There they discovered an uninhabited house with food and drink, as well as comfortable beds, awaiting them. A regular supply of fresh salmon was provided by a device that periodically threw fish into the house from the sea. Similar luxury was encountered on the next isle, which was covered with orchards of delicious apples.

Danger was soon encountered again, however, on islands that were populated by revolving beasts, fighting horses, a mysterious cat and fiery swine. The ground on one

of them was hot like a volcano. Among other strange creatures and encounters on the voyage were gigantic swine and calves so huge that they could not be cooked whole; sheep that changed the colour of their wool apparently at will; a sombre miller who ground everything that was begrudged in the world; a population of mourners; an island divided into four kingdoms by fences made of gold, silver, brass and crystal; a castle with a glass bridge where there lived a beautiful girl who rejected Maeldun's advances; crying birds; a solitary pilgrim on a tiny island that was enlarged every year by divine providence; a wonderful fountain that gushed milk, beer and wine; giant smiths; a sea of glass; a sea of clouds in which castles, forests, animals and a fearsome monster suddenly appeared; an underwater island of prophecy; an amazing water-arch; a gigantic silver column and net, from which the voyagers cut off a small piece as a souvenir; an inaccessible island

MANANNAN MAC LIR, son of the Irish sea god *LIR*, took his name from the Isle of Man, which is situated in the Irish Sea about halfway between Ireland and Britain. Manannan was a sea god, magician and healer, and the ruler of the Land of Promise, where he lived in Emhain ("of the Apple Trees"). His home was imagined to be sited off the western coast of Ireland, somewhere in the Atlantic Ocean. His wife was the renowned beauty *FAND*, who fell in love with the Ulster hero *CUCHULAINN* but finally chose to stay with her sea god husband. Manannan therefore shook a magic cloak between Fand and Cuchulainn in order to make sure they would never meet again.

Manannan Mac Lir was a noble and handsome warrior, who drove a chariot as easily over the waves as over a plain and was said to have a ship that sailed itself. He had both divine and mortal children, and one of his mortal sons, *MONGAN*, was conceived by way of a deception similar to the ruse used for *ARTHUR*'s conception. Manannan slept with an Ulster queen when disguised as her husband. Mongan did, however, inherit supernatural gifts, including the ability to shape-change, and he went on to become a great king and mighty warrior.

MANANNAN, (below), the Irish sea god, rode the waves in a self-propelled boat called "Wave Sweeper". As a sea god, Manannan could stir up or soothe the sea, and help or hinder ships. He often appeared to voyagers, such as Bran, at the outset of their trip. (ILLUSTRATION BY MIRANDA GRAY, 1994.)

MANAWYDAN (above) tried to grow wheat after a mysterious blight had devastated his land. One field was ripe for harvest when overnight it was stripped to the stalks by mice. In despair, he planned to hang one of the mice, until dissuaded by a stranger. (ILLUSTRATION BY ALAN LEE, 1984.)

MARK (below) watches sadly as his wife, Iseult, kneels before a drawn sword, beside herself with grief at Tristan's death. Mark, who was often portrayed as a merciful man, gathered her up and bore her off to a tower where she was restored to health. (ILLUSTRATION BY RUSSELL FLINT, C. 1900.)

MANAWYDAN, son of Llyr, was the Welsh equivalent of the Irish sea god *MANANNAN*, though his links with the sea were far less well defined. The brother of *BRAN THE BLESSED* and *BRANWEN*, he married *RHIANNON* on the death of her husband *PWYLL*. One day he and Rhiannon, along with Rhiannon's son *PRYDERI* and his wife Cigfa, were enveloped in a magical mist. When it cleared, their palace was deserted and the land around it desolate, so they travelled to England, where Manawydan and Pryderi made a living as leatherworkers. So successful were they that the local craftsmen forced them to leave. On their return to Wales, both Pryderi and Rhiannon disappeared by magic, leaving Cigfa and Manawydan alone. He then tried to support them by growing a crop of wheat, but his fields were stripped by mice. He caught one of the mice and would have hanged it, but a passing stranger offered him whatever he wanted in return for the mouse's life. Manawydan asked for the return of Rhiannon and Pryderi. The stranger agreed and revealed himself to be Llwyd, a magician and friend of Gwawl, the suitor whom Rhiannon had refused in order to marry Pwyll. (See also *MAGIC AND ENCHANTMENT*)

MAPONOS see *MABON*.

MARK was the king of Cornwall in the Breton myth of *TRISTAN* and *ISEULT*. He was the guardian of his orphaned nephew Tristan and the husband of Iseult, an Irish princess. Although jealous of Tristan and Iseult, he was not entirely unsympathetic, and even when he came upon the lovers sleeping together with Tristan's sword between them he did not kill them. He exchanged the sword for his own and left without waking them. Shamed by this act of mercy, the lovers knew that they must part. Tristan solemnly returned Iseult to his uncle and went into exile in Brittany.

MATHOLWCH'S (left) convoy of ships glides up to the ragged Welsh shore in the prelude to a doomed marriage between himself and Branwen, the beautiful sister of Bran the Blessed. The ships had ensigns of brocaded silk and an uptilted shield as a sign of peace. (ILLUSTRATION BY ALAN LEE, 1984.)

MEDB (above), the magnificent but malevolent queen of Connacht, was a warrior who fought as fiercely as Morrigan. A wild and wilful woman, she precipitated and perpetuated the bloody war with Ulster in which Cuchulainn and other heroes lost their lives. (ILLUSTRATION BY J LEYENDECKER, 1916.)

MATH was the brother of the Welsh mother goddess *DON* and a great magician. At the time that *PRYDERI* ruled over Dyfed in the southern part of Wales, Math was the lord of Gwynedd in the north. Except during war, Math could only live if his feet were held in the lap of a virgin. When Gilvaethwy, one of his nephews, fell in love with the young woman who held Math's feet in her lap, his brother, *GWYDION*, tricked Math into going to war with Pryderi so that the girl might be left behind. On discovering that he had been deceived, however, the furious Math turned his nephews into animals.

MATHOLWCH, in Welsh mythology, was the Irish king married to *BRANWEN*, the sister of *BRAN THE BLESSED* and half-sister of *EFNISIEN*. Efnisien, because he claimed that he had not been consulted over Branwen's wedding, "cut off the lips of Matholwch's horses at their teeth, their ears to their heads, and their tails to their bodies". Later, when Bran took his army to Ireland to avenge the insult of Branwen being made a cook, Efnisien tossed Matholwch's three-year-old son *GWERN* into a fire. In the battle that followed, nearly all the Britons were killed and all of the Irish except for five pregnant women.

MAXEN see *FABULOUS VOYAGES*

MEDB, also known as Maeve, was the warrior-queen of Connacht. According to Irish mythology, no king could reign in Connacht unless he was married to Medb, who was believed to hold the kingdom's sovereignty in her person. It was also said that she "never was without one man in the shadow of another". Medb's most famous action was the invasion of Ulster, when her forces captured the great brown bull of Cuailgne and killed the Ulster hero *CUCHULAINN*. She was herself slain by Forbai, the son of King *CONCHOBHAR MAC NESSA*, while she was bathing in a pool. Forbai had discovered that Queen Medb was in the habit of regularly taking her bath in a Galway pool. He very carefully measured the exact distance between the spot where she bathed and the shore, then he returned to the Ulster stronghold of Emain Macha and practised with a sling-shot until he was able to knock an apple from the top of a pole over the same distance. Satisfied at last that his aim was perfect, he stealthily made his way back to the pool and hit Queen Medb in the centre of her forehead using his sling-shot. Thus was Ulster revenged.

SINGLE COMBAT

I N WAR, THE ANCIENT CELTS relied on heroic single combat, rather than all-out warfare, as a means of settling disputes. Shortage of manpower forbade multiple pitched battles. Instead, chosen champions, such as Cuchulainn or Morholt, duelled to the death. Even in a large-scale epic war, like the campaign of Cuailgne, the Ulster champion fought in single combat every day with a different warrior. In the Arthurian legends, single combat continued in the form of knightly jousts. While the Celtic heroes wore scant armour, Arthur's mounted knights encased themselves in glittering iron. In addition to the basic weapons of spear, sword, sling and shield, the hero of legend had recourse to magical skills and a range of enchanted weapons, such as Arthur's Excalibur or Fergus Mac Roth's Caladcholg, the original Excalibur.

CUCHULAINN (left), the Irish champion, enjoys a short respite between battles. Exhausted by continual combat, he suffered from chronic lack of sleep, snatching cat-naps between duels. Once, his father Lugh, pitying him, cast the hero into a magical sleep for three days and nights, during which he healed all his wounds. When Cuchulainn defended Ulster alone against the forces of Medb, he confronted chosen champions one by one. Between duels, the restless hero harassed the army with his sling. (ILLUSTRATION BY YVONNE GILBERT, 1994.)

CELTIC CAVALRY (right) ride their battle horses to war, armed with spears and crested helmets. Their comrades on foot wear breeches and caps, and bear spears and long bossed shields, while trumpeters bring up the rear. The Celts were heavily reliant on their long shields, which were usually made of wood and sometimes covered with decorative bronze work. Other sharp-rimmed shields could also be used as missile weapons. (GUNDESTRUP CAULDRON, GILDED SILVER, C. 100 BC.)

GERAINT (left) and the Knight of the Kestrel engage in single combat with such ferocity that they shatter each other's armour. Ostensibly, the duel was over the kestrel, but really Geraint was intent on avenging an insult to Guinevere's handmaiden, made by the knight's dwarf. Goaded on by their seconds, both champions fought tirelessly, until Geraint's rage gave him the edge and he overcame, but spared, the knight. (ILLUSTRATION BY ALAN LEE, 1984.)

OWAIN'S (below) kindness to a lion earned him a faithful friend who proved to be a valiant comrade-in-arms. In this unequal match, the giant was winning until Owain's lion leapt to Owain's defence. When the giant complained that he could handle Owain well enough if it were not for his lion, Owain pushed his pet back into the fortress, but the irrepressible creature leapt over the fortress walls and mauled the giant to death. (ILLUSTRATION BY ALAN LEE, 1984.)

MORGAN LE FAY (above) charmed the unsuspecting Tristram into accepting a beautiful gold shield decorated with a strange motif. The shield's design portrayed a knight, Lancelot, enslaving a royal couple, Arthur and his wife. Innocent of the shield's true motif or motive, Tristram rode to Arthur's court and jousted in the royal tournament. When he duelled with Arthur, the king's spear shattered on the enchanted shield. Such enchanted weapons could help or hinder the best of heroes. (ILLUSTRATION BY AUBREY BEARDSLEY, C. 1870.)

MERLIN, sometimes Myrddin, was the famous wizard of Arthurian mythology. So powerful was his magic that one medieval tradition credits him with the magical construction of Stonehenge, the outstanding British monument that has survived from ancient times. Another of his works was supposed to be King *ARTHUR*'s famous Round Table, a late copy of which can still be seen at Winchester today.

Merlin's birth was the subject of a strange story. Apparently, the Britons were told that a great fortress they had built on Salisbury plain, possibly near Stonehenge, would never be safe until the ground there had been soaked by the blood of a child who had no

MERLIN (below), for all his wisdom, was bewitched by the Lady of the Lake who turned his love to her own ends. She sapped his power and plundered his store of secret knowledge, and when done, she bound him in stone by his own spells. (MERLIN AND NIMUE BY E BURNE-JONES, CANVAS, C. 1870.)

MERLIN (left), sage from another world, was an inspired seer and mystic mage, a wise counsellor and faithful friend to three able kings. This powerful portrayal captures the mystical and visionary nature of Celtic bards, rooted in a deep affinity with nature. (MERLIN BY ALAN LEE, CANVAS, 1984.)

MIDIR (right), one of the Tuatha De Danann, appeared at the palace of Tara to carry off Etain, the Ulster woman he loved, long since lost to him by enchantment. The pair drifted upwards and disappeared through a palace window, and flew to an otherworld. (ILLUSTRATION BY STEPHEN REID, 1910.)

mortal father. Such a half-human sacrifice seemed impossible to achieve, until it was learned that a beautiful girl was with child by a demon. The child turned out to be Merlin, who, though baptized as a Christian, still possessed fabulous powers inherited from his demon father. Somehow the boy did not need to be sacrificed for the sake of the fortress because it is likely that Merlin was able to deal with the

problem by means of magic. Two dragons were, in fact, responsible for the problem.

This mixture of pre-Christian and Christian ideas sits strangely with Merlin's later assistance to King Arthur, whose father *UTHER PENDRAGON* was said to have successfully invaded Britain about this time. Merlin sided with Uther and employed his powers to enable him to sleep with Igraine, the wife of a Cornish nobleman, by disguising him as her husband. Due to this deception Arthur was conceived. Once he ascended the throne, King Arthur had Merlin as his trusted advisor and often used the wizard as a messenger because, as with many of the Celtic gods and goddesses, he could assume any shape he pleased.

There are various accounts of Merlin's death. One tells how the wizard forgot about the seat at the Round Table that only *GALAHAD* could use, being the only knight worthy enough to see the *GRAIL*. Merlin sat down and was at once swallowed up by the earth, like other sinful men who had tried it before him. Another story blames the wizard's death on his passion for women. Either Viviane, possibly the Lady of the Lake, or Nimue, the daughter of a Sicilian siren, imprisoned him in an enchanted wood after Merlin had explained all about the secrets of his own magic. As Merlin told Sir *GAWAIN*, who once

passed by: "I am also the greatest fool. I love another more than I love myself, and I taught my beloved how to bind me to herself, and now no one can set me free." (See also *SAGES AND SEERS; MAGIC AND ENCHANTMENT*)

MIDIR, in Irish mythology, was the proud son of *DAGDA*, father of the gods. Unlike his father, who is usually portrayed as a rough, coarse figure, Midir always appeared as a splendidly dressed young man. Midir's first wife was Fuamnach, the daughter of Beothach. She became furious with jealousy when Midir married a second wife, *ETAIN*, from Ulster. With a druid's aid, Fuamnach turned Etain first into a pool, then into a worm and finally into a fly in order to keep her away from Midir. As a fly Etain was swallowed by the wife of Etar, an Ulster warrior, and reborn as the wife of the High King of Ireland. Although Midir recovered Etain, he had to accept in the end that she was the High King's consort and leave her alone. Midir also had some difficulty in accepting his father's successors as leaders of the *TUATHA DE DANANN*. The conflict that he started seems to have had a dangerously weakening effect on this generation of gods just before the invasion of the Milesians, who then went on to defeat the gods.

MIL OR MILE see *MILESIUS*

MILESIUS sails for Ireland to avenge the death of his nephew, Ith, who was slain by the Tuatha De Danann, rulers of Ireland. Although Milesius did not reach shore himself, his family succeeded, defeating the De Danann who retreated into an invisible otherworld. (ILLUSTRATION BY STEPHEN REID, 1910.)

MILESIUS, sometimes Mil or Mile, was the name given to a Spanish soldier whose sons were said to have organized the final invasion of Ireland. The murder there of their kinsman *ITH* caused the Milesians to take revenge by conquering the island. This they achieved by defeating the *TUATHA DE DANANN*, "the people of the goddess Dana", the existing rulers. Following the final decisive battle between the two forces, which the Milesians won, the Tuatha De Danann retired to an otherworld beneath the soil of Ireland.

MODRED was the treacherous nephew of King *ARTHUR*. While he was away waging war in Brittany, Arthur had appointed Modred his regent, but his scheming nephew tried instead to take the throne and force *GUINEVERE* to marry him. On the king's return, a terrible battle was fought near Salisbury and most of the Knights of the Round Table were killed, including Modred. Arthur, who had been mortally wounded during the battle, was then taken to *AVALON* in a black boat by three mysterious women.

MONGAN was the son of the Manx sea god *MANANNAN MAC LIR*. According to Irish mythology, his conception had been made possible by the use of a deception akin to the one used by *MERLIN* so that *UTHER* could sleep with Igraine and so conceive *ARTHUR*. Manannan Mac Lir had assumed the shape of an Ulster king in order to sleep with his beautiful queen. When Mongan was three days old, his father took him to one of his other-world realms, the Land of Promise, where the boy remained until he had grown to manhood. It is claimed by some traditions that Mongan then returned to Ireland reincarnated as *FIN MACCOOL*, the famous leader of the *FIANNA*, but in other accounts he retained his own identity. The stories about Mongan describe how he used his shape-changing ability to get his own way, and mention in particular the recovery of his wife Dubh Lacha. He had inherited the divine ability of metamorphosis from his father.

MORGAN LE FAY was King *ARTHUR*'s half-sister and in some versions of the story she is said to have been the mistress of Sir Accolon of Gaul. Throughout all the British myths that tell of Arthur's incredible reign Morgan Le Fay is always depicted as the king's implacable enemy, often plotting his downfall. According to one story she is supposed to have stolen the magic sword Excalibur and sent it to Accolon, who then challenged Arthur to single combat. When Accolon dropped the sword Arthur recognized it and the other knight admitted his guilt and surrendered. However, after the bloody battle against Arthur's rebellious nephew Sir *MODRED*, Morgan le Fay was one of the three women who took the grievously wounded king in a black boat to *AVALON*. The other two were "the Queen of Northgales and the Queen of Wastelands". (See also *SAGES AND SEERS; SINGLE COMBAT*)

MODRED (above), Arthur's treacherous nephew, abused his role of regent and usurped the throne, forcing Arthur to quash the rebel forces. Both perished in the final battle that ended the war and so came to an end the Arthurian golden age. (ARTHUR AND MODRED BY W HATHERELL, CANVAS, C.1910.)

MORGAN LE FAY'S (below) paradoxical nature is reflected in her dual role as both healer and dark magician, as Arthur's thorn in life, yet also his guardian in death. Although educated at a convent, she managed to emerge as a gifted magician. (MORGAN LE FAY BY A SANDYS, WOOD, 1864.)

MORHOLT was the gigantic brother of the king of Ireland, to whom King Mark and Cornwall were expected to pay an annual tribute. Mark's nephew *TRISTAN* was determined to put an end to this practice. He therefore sailed to Ireland and succeeded in killing Morholt, but not before he had been wounded by the giant's great poisoned sword. Before he died, Morholt told Tristan that only his sister *ISEULT* would be able to cure his poisoned wound.

MORRIGAN, sometimes known as Morrigu, was an Irish goddess of death on the battlefield who helped the *TUATHA DE DANANN* at both battles of Magh Tuireadh. She was associated with the other war deities *MACHA*, *BADB* and *NEMAIN*. Her favourite form was the crow, and as such she settled in triumph on the shoulder of the Ulster hero *CUCHULAINN* when he was finally killed in the war against Queen *MEDB*'s forces. Cuchulainn had not only refused Morrigan's love, but in anger he had even wounded her. For such a deed his fate was sealed.

MORRIGAN, the terrible goddess of war, appeared sometimes as a warrior in a battle, siding with her favourites. Most often she soared overhead as a raven or crow, shrieking and flapping her wings to scare the host, or to signify imminent death, as here. (ILLUSTRATION BY STEPHEN REID, 1910.)

MORHOLT, the Irish champion, confronts Tristan, the Cornish newcomer, in a duel over Irish taxes. Despite Morholt's greater power and skill, the young Tristan fought like a mighty lion and dealt the older knight a mortal blow to his helm, lodging a piece of sword in his brain. (ILLUSTRATION BY EVELYN PAUL, C. 1900.)

NAOISE was the eldest son of Usna and his wife Elbha, daughter of *CATHBAD*. When *DEIRDRE* persuaded him to run away with her so that she could avoid marriage to the Ulster king *CONCHOBHAR MAC NESSA*, Naoise and his two brothers fled with her to Alba. Conchobhar sent *FERGUS MAC ROTH* to bring them all home. Suspicious of Conchobhar, but trusting Fergus' promise that no harm would come to them, Naoise agreed. In the event, Conchobhar had Naoise killed, and so enraged was Fergus Mac Roth that he joined the forces of Conchobhar's great enemy, Queen *MEDB* of Connacht.

NECHTAN was an Irish water god and, according to some versions, the husband of *BOANN*. On Nechtan's hill there was a holy well that was the source of all knowledge, to which only Nechtan and his three cup-bearers had access. When Boann found her way to the well, the waters rose from the ground and chased after her, becoming the River Boyne.

NEMAIN (whose name means "dreadful" or "venomous"), in Irish mythology, was a goddess of war. Along with *BABD*, *MORRIGAN* and *MACHA*, she formed one of a group of war deities who sometimes appeared as beautiful young women and sometimes as crows, screeching over the battlefield. Nemain was said to have been the wife of *NUADA*, the leader of the *TUATHA DE DANANN*.

NEMGLAN, an Irish bird god, fell in love with Mess Buachalla, the betrothed of Eterscel, High King of Ireland. On the eve of the wedding, Nemglan came to her in a bird skin and seduced her, and this was how she conceived *CONAIRE MOR*. The child was passed off as High King Eterscel's son, but Mess Buachalla was careful to warn the boy that he must never, whatever the circumstances might be, kill a bird. When Conaire Mor was a young man, Eterscel died and the question of the succession was raised in Tara, the Irish capital. Unknown to Conaire, there was a prophecy to the effect that Eterscel's successor would be a naked man walking along the road to Tara with a sling in his hand. It happened one day that Conaire was driving his char-

NAOISE elopes with the great Irish beauty, Deirdre. They fled across the sea to Scotland, pursued by Fergus Mac Roth. By Loch Ness, they found refuge and hunted deer and salmon, living in pastoral bliss until they were lured back to a deadly trap in Ireland by an unsuspecting Fergus Mac Roth. (ILLUSTRATION ANON.)

NEMAIN, one of the dreadful goddesses of war, appeared sometimes as a washer at the ford, presaging doom. Before his last combat, Cuchulainn saw a washer weeping and wailing as she rinsed a heap of bloody raiment belonging to the great hero. (ILLUSTRATION BY STEPHEN REID, 1910.)

iot down this very road when a flock of birds with beautiful plumage descended upon him. Forgetting his mother's instruction never to harm any bird, he loaded his sling, at which point the birds immediately turned into armed warriors. The leader of these incredible warriors, however, introduced himself to Conaire as his real father Nemglan. To make up for his misconduct towards the birds, Conaire was told to undress and return home to Tara on foot, carrying only his sling. He thus became the next High King of Ireland.

NESSA, in Irish mythology, was the mother of *CONCHOBHAR MAC NESSA*, the Ulster ruler during the lifetime of the hero *CUCHULAINN*. Nessa's husband was King Fachtna of Ulster and when the king died his half-brother, *FERGUS MAC ROTH*, succeeded to the throne and proposed marriage to Nessa.

However, she would agree to the match only on the condition that her son should be allowed to rule Ulster for one year. Fergus Mac Roth was so in love with her that he readily agreed, but at the end of the year the people of Ulster refused to let Conchobhar step down from the throne, so excellent was his rule.

NEMGLAN, *a bird god from an other-world, came to Mess Buachalla before her wedding to the High King. As he flew in, his plumage moulted to reveal a beautiful youth. Like Leda and Danae before her, she loved the god and bore him a son, Conaire Mor. (ILLUSTRATION BY NICK BEALE, 1995.)*

NIAMH

NIAMH was the wife of CONALL Caernach. While CUCHULAINN was recovering from wounds sustained during the war against the men of Connacht, Niamh nursed him and became his mistress. She then tried to prevent him returning to battle. But the witch BADB, one of the daughters of CALATIN, cast a spell on Niamh so that she wandered away into the countryside. Badb then assumed the form of Niamh and told Cuchulainn that he must return to the war and fight.

NIAM OF THE GOLDEN HAIR

NIAM OF THE GOLDEN HAIR was a daughter of the sea god MANANNAN MAC LIR. She fell in love with the poet OISIN and they lived happily together in the Land of Promise, which was one of the otherworld realms. Niam bore the poet a daughter, Plur nam Ban ("Flower of Woman").

NODENS

NODENS was a British god of healing, whose magic hounds were also believed to be able to cure the sick. Nodens was worshipped during the Roman occupation; the ruins of a great temple have been found on the banks of the River Severn. In Ireland, he became NUADA of the Silver Hand and in Wales NUDD of the Silver Hand, also known as Llud to the Britons.

NUADA

NUADA, also known as Nuada Airgetlamh ("Nuada of the Silver Hand"), because of a temporary replacement for a hand he lost at the first battle of Magh Tuireadh, was an important Irish god and leader of the TUATHA DE DANANN. He was married to NEMAIN. The De Danann were a younger generation of gods than the FOMORII, the sea gods who were soon to challenge them at the second battle of Magh Tuireadh. For a while between the two battles, Nuada appointed BRES as leader because of the loss of his hand. The silver replacement was made by DIAN CECHT. But Nuada was dissatisfied with it and turned to Dian Cecht's son Miach, who made him a new hand of flesh and blood. Dian Cecht slew Miach out of jealousy. Nuada's restoration as leader caused the second battle of Magh Tuireadh, because the half-Fomorii Bres complained to his kinsmen about his treatment.

At the second battle the lethal eye of BALOR killed both Nuada and Nemain before the sun god LUGH destroyed it with a sling-shot. Their victory saved the Tuatha De Danann, but later they in turn were defeated by the sons of MILESIUS. That Nuada was the great De Danann leader, there is no doubt. He is described as sitting on his throne "with a white light about him as it had been a fleece of silver, and round his head a wheel of light pulsed and beat with changing colours". Nuada is cognate with the Welsh NUDD.

NUDD

NUDD, known as Llud to the British, is the Welsh equivalent of NUADA. He also had a silver hand, and in one tale was known as Llud Llawereint ("silver-handed").

NUDD, *or Llud, ruled Britain at a time when it was plagued by a strange May Eve scream. It transpired that two subterranean dragons caused the scream during an annual battle. They were soothed by sinking mead into a pit dug through the centre of the earth. (ILLUSTRATION BY ALAN LEE, 1984.)*

OGMA was the Irish god of eloquence and the inventor of Ogham, the earliest system of writing used in Ireland. Ogham is made up of a series of vertical or sloping lines inscribed on a base line. The sagas tell of vast libraries of Ogham writing, though only inscriptions in stone carvings have survived, and the sagas themselves were later recorded by monks using the Roman alphabet.

Ogma was a son of *DAGDA*, who was a god described as the "Lord of Knowledge". Besides having a truly remarkable skill as a poet, Ogma was a fighter like other Irish gods and also, like the the Greek god Hermes or the Roman Mercury, he was responsible for conveying souls to the otherworld. Whereas for the Greek and Roman messenger gods this was a sad duty, not least because the kingdom of Hades was not an inviting place, Ogma's task was a happier one since the Celtic otherworld was a delightful and peaceful resting-place for the soul prior to its next rebirth in the world. It is thought that Greek colonists in the western end of the

OISIN and the fairy maiden, Niamh, flew away on a snow-white steed through golden mist to the Land of Promise, which was a delightful otherworld beyond all dreams, filled with birdsong and scented flowers, with overflowing mead and wondrous creatures. (ILLUSTRATION BY STEPHEN REID, 1910.)

OGMA, god of eloquence, invented the Ogham script, consisting of vertical lines crossing a lateral baseline. Ogham messages were carved on stone and inscribed on barks and wands of hazel or aspen. Over 400 ancient messages have survived. (ILLUSTRATION BY NICK BEALE, 1995.)

Mediterranean first encountered the idea of the transmigration of souls from their Celtic neighbours. In the sixth century BC the famous and unusual Greek philosopher Pythagoras left the Aegean island of Samos and went to live in the city of Croton in southern Italy. He became extremely interested in the theory of reincarnation. His followers, who believed that the soul was immortal, accepted transmigration through animals and plants as well, and as a result proposed the kinship of all living things.

In some Irish myths Ogma is said to have married *ETAIN*, who was the daughter of the god of healing *DIAN CECHT*. At the second and final battle of Magh Tuireadh Ogma slew Indech, son of the *FOMORII* goddess Domnu. Indech was one of the leaders of the Fomorii, who were the older sea gods who had challenged the *TUATHA DE DANANN*, the younger generation of gods of which Ogma was one. After the terrible battle was over and the De Danann were victorious, Ogma claimed as his prize a magic Fomorii sword that was capable of recounting all the deeds it had performed.

OISIN, sometimes Ossian, was the son of the Fenian, or *FIANNA*, leader *FINN MACCOOL*. According to Irish mythology, Oisin was the greatest poet in Ireland, perhaps not a surprising achievement considering how as a young man his father had eaten the Salmon of Knowledge. Oisin's mother was none other than the goddess *SADB*, the granddaughter of *DAGDA*. This made *OGMA*, the god of eloquence, Oisin's uncle.

One day, as Finn MacCool with his companions and dogs was returning homewards, a beautiful deer started up on their path and the ensuing chase took them towards Tara, the Irish capital and the base of the Fenians. At last the exhausted animal stopped and crouched down on the ground, but instead of attacking their quarry the hounds began to play round her, and even to lick her head and limbs. So Finn MacCool ordered that no harm should be done to the deer, which followed them on the way home until sunset.

That same night Finn MacCool awoke to find the most beautiful woman he had ever seen standing next to his bed. It was Sadb. She

explained how a spell had been placed upon her, but that she had learned that if Finn MacCool came to love her, then all the enchantments would cease to have power and she could resume her normal shape. So it came to pass that Sadb lived with Finn MacCool as his mistress, and for months neither of them stirred from their dwelling. Then news arrived of invaders in ships off Dublin, most likely a Viking raid, and the Fenians were called to arms. For only one week Finn MacCool was absent dealing with the Vikings. On his return, however, he discovered that Sadb had been lured away by someone disguised as himself (a common trick among shape-changers in Irish mythology). Realizing that it must be the enchanter whom Sadb had rejected, Finn MacCool organized a search of every remote hill, valley and forest in the country, but without success. Eventually he gave up all hope of finding his mistress and returned to his pleasure of hunting. It happened, by chance, that his dogs tracked down a very strange quarry and Finn MacCool came upon them surrounding a naked boy with long hair. His two best hounds were, in fact, keeping the pack from seizing the child.

Having driven off the dogs, Finn MacCool and the other huntsmen regarded the boy with curiosity. He told them that he did not know the identity of his father, but that his mother was a gentle hind, with whom he lived in a quiet valley safely shut in by steep cliffs. To their home a tall, dark stranger came every now and again to see his mother, but she always shrank away in fear and the man left in anger. When the stranger finally

OISIN *returned from the otherworld after his time and found himself an old man, alone and bereft, the sole survivor of a magical age. With his lyre he sang of the heroes and gods of his era, conjuring up the magical phantoms of that bygone age.*
(OSSIAN *BY* FRANCOIS GERARD, *CANVAS, 1800.*)

His famous adventure concerns *NIAMH*, the daughter of the sea god *MANANNAN MAC LIR*. Oisin met her while on a hunt by the shores of a lake. She suddenly appeared riding a horse with silver hooves and a golden mane. When Niamh told Oisin how she had travelled a great distance to invite him to her father's otherworld realm, the Land of Promise, he readily mounted the magic steed and was never seen by his father again. In the otherworld kingdom he fought against a *FOMORII* giant in an undersea combat worthy of his father. But after a number of other exploits Oisin began to miss his own land of Ireland. Niamh gave him her magic horse so that he could visit his home, but told him not to dismount otherwise he would never be allowed to return. Ireland appeared to Oisin almost a strange land, for everyone he knew had died long before. The people seemed far sadder and more care-worn than the heroes he had grown up with. By chance he came upon a ragged group of men attempting to move a boulder, which he easily lifted for them while still seated on his mount. However, his saddle slipped and he fell to the ground. In an instant the magic horse vanished and the valiant young warrior was turned into a blind and frail old man.

A Christian addition to the end of this myth includes St Patrick. Because everyone took Oisin to be mad he cried out: "If your god has slain Finn MacCool, then I would say that he is a strong man." So he was taken to the saint, who recorded his strange tale and explained the changes to Ireland since the arrival of Christianity.

struck her with a magic hazel wand, the hind was forced to follow him, although she tried to comfort her son as she left.

As soon as the boy finished this account, Finn MacCool embraced him as his own son by Sadb, and immediately named him Oisin ("Little Fawn"). He was trained as a Fenian warrior, which involved one of the most difficult courses of training imaginable, and became a skilled fighter like his father, but he also inherited the gentler ability of eloquence from his mother, and his songs and poetry were admired throughout Ireland.

OISIN, *on his return from the otherworld, found Ireland bleak and cold, the people sad and small, and himself a weary and withered old man. After passing on the magic legends, he quietly slipped away, his end as strange as his beginning.*
(ILLUSTRATION *BY* STEPHEN REID, *1910.*)

HEROIC QUESTS

THE THRILLING PURSUIT of a real or visionary goal forms the plot of many compelling tales of adventure. The goal is not always the most tantalizing part of the venture and might seem like a tedious or even trivial task, but serves to spur the traveller on his way. Other goals, such as the Grail, seem barely attainable, but serve as shining symbols of aspiration. The impetus is sometimes romantic, as when Culhwch set out to find fair Olwen; or retributory, as when Geraint went forth to avenge a wrong; while Peredur, Owain and the Grail Knights were inspired by otherworldly visions and ideals. Whatever the goal, the quest usually takes on a magic of its own, leading the hero down unexpected bypaths of adventure and discovery. *En route* he meets new friends and travelling companions, learns much-needed lessons and catches sight of even more tantalizing quests ahead.

OWAIN (above), inspired by the tale of Cynon, set off in search of the Castle of the Fountain, which was guarded by the Black Knight. He passed through the fairest vale until he saw a shining castle on the hill. After entering its otherworldly domain Culhwch defeated the Black Knight, and went on to woo his widow. After a rather difficult beginning, he overcame her resentment, and guarded her realm until his yen for adventure lured him off again. (ILLUSTRATION BY ALAN LEE, 1984.)

CAMELOT (left), Arthur's shining city-castle, drew knights from far and wide to join the Fellowship of the Round Table, inspired by ideals of courage, honour and vision. From Camelot, the questing knight set forth on journeys of adventure and discovery, to seek honour, to avenge wrongs and to win ladies and renown. The figure of the questing knight became a symbol of aspiration. (ILLUSTRATION BY ALAN LEE, 1984.)

THE GRAIL QUEST (right) proved to be the hardest, highest and greatest of all quests. Many knights set forth but few returned. When Arthur's warriors resolved to undertake the Grail Quest, Arthur wept, lamenting that the fairest fellowship of noble knights would never meet again around the table at Camelot. He was right, for few of his company were fitted for the quest and many perished. (THE ARMING AND DEPARTURE OF THE KNIGHTS BY E BURNE-JONES AND W MORRIS, TAPESTRY, 1895–96.)

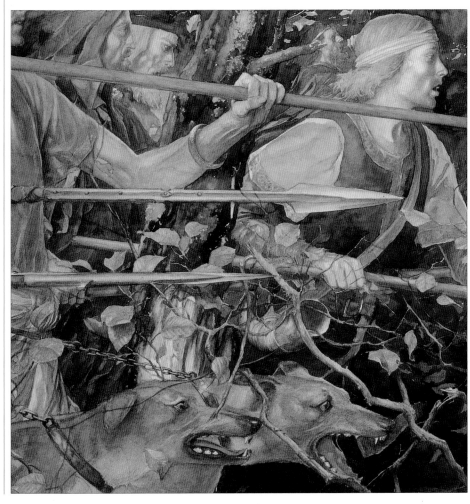

CULHWCH'S (left) quest for the fair Olwen involved thirty-nine impossible tasks, the longest series of tasks in Celtic mythology. En route the hero enlisted the help of Arthur's war-band who assisted Culhwch in one of his hardest tasks, which was the retrieval of a comb, razor and scissors from between the ears of the terrible, enchanted boar, Twrch Trwyth. (ILLUSTRATION BY ALAN LEE, 1984.)

PEREDUR'S (above) quest for adventure led him through many wondrous lands. At one point he passed through a lovely river valley, filled with colourful pavilions and a wondrous multitude of windmills and water-mills. He lodged with the head miller and jousted in the tournament, defeating countless warriors with such skill and might that he impressed the local empress. After fighting her battles, he ruled with her for fourteen years before continuing his search for new adventures. (ILLUSTRATION BY ALAN LEE, 1984.)

OLWEN, in Welsh mythology, was the daughter of the giant Yspaddaden and her suitor was *CULHWCH*, one of King *ARTHUR*'s warriors. Culhwch's stepmother hated him so much that she cursed him to marry only Olwen, a girl whom the warrior came to love dearly. Yspaddaden was so upset by the obvious affection between Olwen and Culhwch that he set his daughter's lover a series of tasks in order to prevent the marriage. Among other things, Culhwch had to uproot a forest, burn the wood for fertilizer and plough the cleared land in one day; force *AMAETHON*, the god of agriculture, to nourish its crops; make the smith god Govannon forge tools for the work; bring four strong oxen to help; obtain magic seed; provide honey nine times sweeter than that of a virgin swarm; get a magic cup and a hamper of delicious meat; borrow the drinking-horn of the under-water king Gwyddbwyll and the magic harp belonging to Teirtu (an instrument that played itself); capture the birds of *RHIANNON*, whose song could wake the dead and lull the living to sleep; provide a magic cauldron; a boar's tusk for the giant to shave with and shaving cream made from a witch's blood;

OWAIN and Arthur (below) appear in a warrior's dream, playing gwyddbwyll. During the game, Arthur's knights battle with Owain's ravens, but the players simply play on, until Arthur smashes the pieces. The game symbolizes a battle, possibly for sovereignty. (ILLUSTRATION BY ALAN LEE, 1984.)

steal a magic dog, leash and collar; hire as a huntsman *MABON*, son of Modron, who had first to be released from prison; find a wonderful steed and swift hounds; steal a comb, scissors and a razor from between the ears of a fierce boar; and persuade a number of unlikely guests to come to Yspaddaden's stronghold. Undaunted by the

OLWEN (left), in flaming red, wanders through the otherworld, depicted here as a vibrant, brooding wooded idyll. Olwen was loved by Culhwch, a warrior of King Arthur's court, who had to go to great lengths to secure his bride.
(ILLUSTRATION BY ALAN LEE, 1984.)

sheer size and complexity of the challenges, Culhwch said that "King Arthur will provide horses and men to help him win Olwen". He also informed the giant that he would return to slay him. Culhwch succeeded and married Olwen "and she was his only wife as long as he lived". The giant was killed by one of Culhwch's fellow knights.

OWAIN (below) peers through the tangled branches of the wildwood, like a shy, wild creature. Overcome with shame after wronging his wife, he fled into the wilderness and lived as a wild man, wasting away until rescued by a noblewoman.
(ILLUSTRATION BY ALAN LEE, 1984.)

PARTHOLON (above) found a lush, primal country when he first landed in Ireland. The forests and plains were alive with strange, shy and beautiful creatures. Partholon cleared the land for cultivation and in his time three new lakes appeared, one of which was named after his son. (ILLUSTRATION BY ARTHUR RACKHAM, C. 1910.)

OSCAR, in Irish mythology, was the son of *OISIN* and the grandson of *FINN MACCOOL*. His name means "deer lover" and recalls his grandmother, the goddess *SADB*, whom Finn MacCool first encountered while he was hunting. Sadb had been changed into a hind by a spell, which Finn MacCool briefly lifted. Oscar's mother was Eibhir, who was said to be "a yellow-haired maiden from a warm country".

Oscar was a mighty fighter, one of the best of all the *FIANNA*, or Fenians, the warriors who acted as a bodyguard to the High King of Ireland. But he lived during a time when the ruler, Cairbe, felt that the Fenians had too much power, and a bloody struggle ensued. High King Cairbe refused to pay the Fenians for their services and raised another band of fighters to replace them. In a battle fought at Gabhra, near present-day Dublin, Oscar killed Cairbe in single combat but was himself mortally wounded. According to one version of the myth, Finn MacCool returned briefly from the otherworld to mourn Oscar's death.

OWAIN, in Welsh mythology, was the son of *URIEN* and one of King *ARTHUR*'s warriors. When a fellow warrior named *CYNON* was defeated by a mysterious Black Knight, Owain set out to find this stranger. He severely wounded the Black Knight but did not unseat him, and when the knight galloped off to a nearby castle, he gave chase only to find himself almost a prisoner once he entered its walls. Owain was saved by a lady named Luned, who gave him a ring of invisibility. Soon the lord of the castle, the Black Knight, died of the wound Owain had inflicted on him. Not deterred by her grief, Owain persuaded Luned to plead his cause with such success that his widow consented to marry him. Thus he became master of the Castle of the Fountain, as the Black Knight's stronghold was called. But the long absence of Owain worried King Arthur a great deal, so he sent out a party of knights to find him. Owain returned with them to King Arthur's court, and he gradually forgot about his wife.

When a very angry lady arrived at court to accuse Owain of deceit, treachery and unfaithfulness, he was overcome with shame. A remorseful Owain fled to the forest and pursued the solitary life of a hermit. There he would have died but for a well-born lady who used a magic potion to restore his health. Sir Owain took up his arms, slew a dragon and befriended a lion. The knight and the lion had numerous adventures, which included saving Luned from death by burning and slaying a giant. Owain returned to the Castle of the Fountain, where he was reconciled with his wife. They seem to have spent the rest of their lives together in King Arthur's court. (See also *CELTIC ROMANCE; SINGLE COMBAT; HEROIC QUESTS*)

PARSIFAL see *PERCIVAL*

PARTHOLON, son of Sera, was believed to have led one of the early invasions of Ireland. Together with twenty-four men and their wives, he is said to have come out of the west after the waters of the Flood had receded and cleared the island of trees ready for cultivation. According to the myth, after living in Ireland for some five thousand years, the race of Partholon were stricken by disease and they all died within the space of a week.

PELLES was one of the names given to the "Maimed King" of the *GRAIL* story in whose castle of Carbonek the holy vessel was kept. In other versions of the tale he is known as Amfortas. Pelles was said to have been the father of Elaine, who fell in love with Sir *LANCELOT* and bore him the pure knight Sir *GALAHAD*, who was the only one of *ARTHUR*'s knights granted a vision of the Grail and allowed to hold it.

PELLES, the Grail King, guarded the Grail in Carbonek, the Grail Castle. Maimed by an incurable wound, symbolizing some spiritual imperfection, he lived in a twilight state, while his country wasted, awaiting the coming of Galahad, the redeeming knight. (ILLUSTRATION BY ALAN LEE, 1984.)

PERCIVAL, the Perfect Fool, attained a glimpse of the Grail through his innocence. Returning from Sarras, he became Grail King, heading the Order of Grail Knights, sometimes known as Parsifal, sometimes as Templeisen, after the Knights Templar.
(PARZIVAL BY MARTIN WIEGAND, CANVAS, 1934.)

PERCIVAL, who was also sometimes called Perceval or Parsifal in different traditions, was in later Arthurian mythology something of an outsider. He was brought up in a forest far from the court of Camelot and was completely ignorant of courtly manners. However, he travelled to King *ARTHUR*'s court and was duly made a knight, and then set off in quest of the Grail, the holy vessel that was used at the Last Supper and which received the blood that flowed from the spear thrust in Christ's side at the time of the Crucifixion. The Grail had been brought to Britain by *JOSEPH OF ARIMATHEA*, the rich man who had allowed Christ's body to be placed in his tomb. However, the Grail was later lost and its recovery became the great quest for the Knights of the Round Table.

The purity of Sir Percival may have meant that he was permitted a brief glimpse of the Grail, but he was denied the complete vision and heavenly release that was eventually granted to Sir *GALAHAD*, Sir *LANCELOT*'s son. Only Galahad was allowed to touch the Grail, "Our Lord's body between his hands", and then to die in the company of angels. The mysterious Queen of the Wastelands, one of the three ladies who took the dying King Arthur to *AVALON* after he had been wounded in the battle against *MODRED*, was Sir Percival's aunt. On his personal quest for the Grail, Sir Percival unfortunately fell somewhat short of the high standard of conduct required for recovering the Grail. One day on his journey he encountered a wondrous and mysterious ship and at once fell in love with its beautiful owner. Indeed, he was on the point of entering her bed when, "by chance and grace, Sir Percival saw his unsheathed sword lying on the ground, and on its pommel was a red cross, the sign of the Crucifixion, which reminded him of his knightly duty to behave as a good man. So he made the sign of the cross on his forehead, at which the boat was upended, then changed into a cloud of black smoke." So annoyed and filled with remorse was Percival by this moral lapse that he felt obliged to inflict a punishment on the weakness of his own flesh by wounding himself in the thigh. Meanwhile, the enchantress who had attempted to waylay him and divert him from his quest "set off with the wind roaring and yelling, that it seemed all the water was burned after her".

PEREDUR, in Welsh mythology, was the seventh son of Evrawg and the only surviving male. His father and brothers were killed before his own coming of age. This did not prevent Peredur from becoming one of *ARTHUR*'s warriors and his many adventures formed the basis for the later stories about *PERCIVAL*. Possibly because of his position as a seventh son, always a significant

PEREDUR, raised in rustic secrecy, grew up strong and agile but devoid of courtly manners. When he saw three shining knights, he was entranced. Devising a saddle of twigs, and armed with a sharpened stake, he set forth for Arthur's court. (ILLUSTRATION BY ALAN LEE, 1984.)

number, Peredur was particularly adept at defeating witches, who in Wales took to the field like knights attired in full armour. Indeed, his myth as it is told in the *Mabinogion* ends with a terrible duel between him and a leading witch. "For the third time the hag slew a man of Arthur's before Peredur's eyes, and Peredur drew his sword and smote the witch on the crest of her helmet so that the helmet and all the armour were split into two. And she raised a shout, and ordered the rest of the witches to flee, and said it was Peredur who was destined to slay all the witches of Caer Loyw." (See also *HEROIC QUESTS*)

PRYDERI, in Welsh mythology, was the son of *PWYLL*, a notable chieftain of Dyfed in south Wales, and of *RHIANNON*. Pryderi was snatched from his cot by one of

Rhiannon's rejected suitors and brought up by *TEIRNON*, a chieftain who discovered the infant in his stable. The chieftain's wife named the child Gwri, or "Golden Hair", but when, after seven years, he was finally returned home, Rhiannon renamed him Pryderi, "Care", because during the child's absence her life had been very careworn. She had been falsely accused of killing her son and was made to do penance by sitting at the gate of Pwyll's fortress and telling strangers of her crime, then offering to carry them on her back into her hall.

When Pwyll died, Pryderi succeeded him as lord of Dyfed and gave his mother in marriage to *MANAWYDAN*, son of the Welsh sea god Llyr, although in Pryderi's myth Manawydan appears as a mortal warrior rather than a god. At their wedding banquet there was a peal of thunder and a mist fell. "No one could see the other, although the great hall was filled with light." When the mist cleared, the land was desolate. People, animals and crops were gone. Pryderi, his wife Cigfa, Manawydan and Rhiannon were the only people left. After two

years eking out an existence on wild honey, fish and game, they finally decided to travel across the border to Lloegyr, present-day England. But the skill of Manawydan and Pryderi as craftsmen made them many enemies and they returned to Wales. In a ruined castle, Pryderi came across a golden bowl fastened by four chains on a marble slab. Pryderi went to pick it up, but his hands stuck to the bowl and he found that he could not move or let it go. He was also struck dumb. When his mother tried to save him, Rhiannon and Pryderi disappeared in another mist.

It later emerged that all the strange events had been caused by a spell laid on the household by an enemy of Pwyll, Pryderi's father. Manawydan discovered the truth as he was about to hang a mouse for eating their corn. The creature turned out to be the wife of Llwyd, the old enemy of Pwyll. Other mice helping to devour the crops were his warriors transformed by magic. During their temporary disappearance, Pryderi and his mother had been forced to work as donkeys.

PEREDUR aroused the rage of the Pride of the Clearing when he supped with his wife. The arrogant knight assumed his wife's guilt and punished her until Peredur finally challenged and overthrew him. Here, splendid as a peacock, the proud one rides out to joust with Peredur. (ILLUSTRATION BY ALAN LEE, 1984.)

PRYDERI, lord of Dyfed, marched into Gwynedd to avenge the theft of his swine by the resourceful magician, Gwydion. The dispute was to be decided by single combat, but the match was unequal as Gwydion bewitched Pryderi with magical illusions. (ILLUSTRATION BY ALAN LEE, 1984.)

at last, because when the baby was stolen her maids were so afraid of Pwyll that they blamed Rhiannon. They laid bones next to their sleeping mistress and smeared her face and hands with blood. When Rhiannon awoke in amazement, the maids told Pwyll how she had devoured the baby in the night.

Pwyll imposed a humiliating penance upon her. Every day she had to sit by his gate, tell her tale to every stranger who came and offer to carry them on her back to the great hall. Not until the eventual return of her son, whom she called *PRYDERI* ("Care"), was Rhiannon excused from her penance. (See also *CELTIC OTHERWORLDS; MAGIC AND ENCHANTMENT*)

RHIANNON, in Welsh mythology, was the daughter of Hereydd, and the long-suffering wife of *PWYLL*, a chieftan of Dyfed. All of Rhiannon's troubles stemmed from her rejection of Gwawl, the man to whom she had been promised, and as a result his enraged father had laid a spell on Pwyll's household.

Because of this curse, Rhiannon suffered years of barrenness and, after the birth of a son, she was unjustly accused of eating the baby. Even after the boy, whom she named *PRYDERI*, which meant "Care", had been restored and grown up, the spell continued to dog Rhiannon. At one stage she and Pryderi were changed into donkeys. Rhiannon herself had her own magical aspect, however, for the singing of her birds was said to be able to wake the dead and send the living to sleep.

Rhiannon is a singular figure in Welsh mythology. She bore her suffering and injustice with a patience that still seems remarkable. But her real nature was in all likelihood originally connected

RHIANNON (below), as first seen by Pwyll, was a vision in white and gold, riding a pearly steed, and clad in brocaded silk. The two seemed made for each other, but a curse clouded their love and marriage. As patient as she was beautiful, Rhiannon endured her lot without complaint. (ILLUSTRATION BY ALAN LEE, 1984.)

PWYLL was a chieftain of Dyfed whose authority even reached into *ANNWN*, the Welsh otherworld. Indeed, he boasted the title Pen Annwn ("Lord of Beyond"). One day Pwyll was hunting in the forest when he saw an unusual pack of hounds running down a stag. These hounds were snow-white in colour and had red ears. Pwyll drove them off and was setting his own pack on the cornered stag when a grey-clad horseman rode up and accused him of discourtesy for chasing away his hounds. Pwyll accepted the charge and promised to make amends, at which the stranger revealed himself to be *ARAWN*, the ruler of Annwn. Arawn told Pwyll that he was being harried by a rival named Havgan, who could be slain only by a single blow, since a second one immediately revived him. Pwyll agreed to change places and shapes with Arawn for a

PWYLL (above), disguised as a beggar, lies in wait with 100 horsemen to trick Gwawl, a rival suitor for the hand of Rhiannon. Once overpowered, Gwawl agreed to leave the two in peace, but his bitter curse blighted their marriage with strange misfortunes. (ILLUSTRATION BY ALAN LEE, 1984.)

year, and to slay Havgan. During the period of exchange it was understood that Pwyll would not make love to Arawn's wife, even though he would share her bed.

Pwyll, having successfully killed Havgan and fulfilled his promise to Arawn, returned home. He then wooed and won *RHIANNON* for his wife, although a rival suitor never forgave him and laid a curse upon his household, both before and after Pwyll's death. For years no child was born and, angered at her barrenness, Pwyll treated Rhiannon unkindly. His attitude became worse after she gave birth to a son

RHIANNON'S singing birds were heralds of the otherworld. Their beautiful and enchanting song was said to be able to wake the dead and to lull the living into a deep sleep. Celtic art and myth are alive with birds of every kind. While some, such as ravens, presage doom, swans and singing birds heal with their magical song.
(ILLUSTRATION ANON.)

RUADH, an intrepid voyager, discovered a secret island beneath the waves, on which lived nine beautiful women who slept on nine bronze beds. Their eyes shone with rainbow light, bewitching Ruadh for nine blissful nights before he grew restless again.
(ILLUSTRATION BY NICK BEALE, 1995.)

with horses. When Pwyll first set eyes on her, Rhiannon was riding "a big fine pale white horse, covered with a garment of shining gold brocaded silk". Also, Rhiannon's stolen son was found in a stable and her punishment for losing him was to act as a beast of burden to visitors who came to her husband's palace. It is tempting to link her with the horse goddess *EPONA*, one of the few Celtic gods or goddesses to be worshipped by the Romans.

RONAN, king of Leinster, was, in the tangled relations of his second marriage, the Irish equivalent of the great Greek hero Theseus. Just like Theseus' second wife Phaedra, the king's second wife Eochaid loved Ronan's son more than her husband. When the stepson showed his horror of her passion, Eochaid told her husband that the young man had attempted to rape her. Ronan ordered his son's execution and died of remorse when he later learned the truth. Eochaid ended her own life with poison.

RUADAN, in Irish mythology, was the son of the goddess *BRIGID* and of *BRES*, the half-*FOMORII* ruler

SADB, a gentle goddess, was compelled by an evil druid to live much of her life as a deer. However, she bore Finn MacCool a lovely son, from whose tiny forehead grew a tuft of deer hair where she had licked the boy, giving rise to his name, "Little Fawn".
(ILLUSTRATION BY ARTHUR RACKHAM, C. 1910.)

of the *TUATHA DE DANANN*. At the second battle of Magh Tuireadh Ruadan was sent to spy on the Tuatha De Danann smith god *GOIBHNIU* who was busily making spears. Ruadan seized one of these weapons and thrust it into the god, but Goibhniu merely pulled it out again and drove it into Ruadan, mortally wounding him. When the goddess Brigid came to the battle-field to bewail her son, her weeping was said to have been the first keening in Ireland.

RUADH was a voyager whose ship became becalmed off the north coast of Ireland. According to Irish mythology, when he swam away to find help for his dying crew, he chanced upon a magical underwater island. On the island there lived nine beautiful women, and for nine wonderful nights Ruadh slept with all of them. The women then informed him that together they would bear him a son. Although Ruadh promised faithfully to return at the end of his voyage, he unfortunately forgot about his underwater lovers, and they, in their fury, pursued him, kicking the severed head of his son before them like a football.

SADB, in Irish mythology, was the mistress of *FINN MACCOOL*, the great leader of the *FIANNA*, popularly known as the Fenians, the bodyguard of the High King. She first appeared to the hero while he was out hunting, but although a goddess herself, Sadb had been placed under a powerful spell by a wizard and was compelled to take the form of a deer. That night, however, Sadb came to Finn as a woman and for a time they lived happily together. Then, when Finn was away from home, the wizard returned and turned Sadb into a deer again. Finn searched the whole of Ireland for his lost mistress, but the only trace he found of her was a naked boy who had been raised in the wild. The hero recognized him as his own son by Sadb, so he called him *OISIN*, meaning "Little Fawn". Oisin grew up to become one of the most famous of all Irish poets.

FABULOUS VOYAGES

THE EPIC VOYAGES of Celtic myth are fabulous tours of the otherworld, usually through an archipelago of wonder isles. The yen to travel itself was often inspired by tales of the otherworld, and the epic trips of both Bran and Brendan were sparked off by otherworldly visions. Like another intrepid voyager, Maeldun, they sailed across the oceans, exploring a myriad of dreamlike isles, some of timeless delights and some of deadly perils. Like time travellers, Celtic voyagers experienced a time warp, either returning home long after their time or condemned to wander on a journey without end. Another feature of the restless Celtic voyager was his eventual disenchantment with otherworldly delights, and a yearning for the changing seasons of his homeland.

MAELDUN (left) set sail to avenge his father's murder and, en route, passed through a fabulous archipelago. In one striking episode, he reached an island surmounted by a fortress with a brazen door and a glass drawbridge which threw the travellers backwards – a telling sign of the otherworld. When they struck the bronze door, a soporific sound sent them to sleep until they awoke to the welcoming voice of the castle's enchantress. When Maeldun tried to woo her, the whole castle dissolved, and the sailors found themselves at sea again. (ILLUSTRATION BY ALAN LEE, 1984.)

BRAN'S (above) voyage was sparked off by a blossoming and scented silver fairy bough, left beside him as he slept. Later a beautiful woman clad in otherworldly robes came to reclaim the bough; she sang a lay about her lovely home across the sea which inspired Bran and his kinsmen to set sail. Far out to sea, they reached her wondrous isle of blossoming trees, just one of 50 such delightful heavens where people lived in timeless joy and plenty. Yet all too soon, Bran's crew craved the changing seasons of their homeland. (ILLUSTRATION BY DANUTA MEYER, 1994.)

A DREAM (below) of a fabulous voyage inspired the Roman ruler, Maxen, to set off on an epic voyage from Rome to Britain, in search of the lovely isle and even lovelier woman of his dream. He passed through river valleys and scaled mountains with their summits lost in heaven. Beyond, he reached a great harbour filled with beautiful ships. Picking the loveliest, crafted in silver, gold and ivory, he sailed across the wide sea until he reached the sparkling shores of Cornwall. Within a jewelled fortress, he found the lovely woman of his dream. (ILLUSTRATION BY ALAN LEE, 1984.)

BRIAN (above) and his brothers set off on a perilous mission to find eight objects deposited around the world. They voyaged in "Wave Sweeper", the self-propelled boat of Manannan, across the oceans to Greece and Persia. One task was to find an inexhaustible cooking spit, which was kept by sea nymphs on the sunken isle of Finchory. Brian, in a magical water suit, sank down among 150 maidens and seized the golden spit from the hearth of their underwater castle. (ILLUSTRATION BY STEPHEN REID, 1912.)

BRENDAN (above), an intrepid Irish monk inspired by tales of the Land of Promise, set sail on an epic voyage. Like Maeldun, he reached an island of bird-like spirits, possibly the Land of Promise, and crossed a translucent sea. Unlike Maeldun, he landed on an island which moved when he lit a fire and turned out to be the giant whale, Jasconius. Here, the dauntless saint tames a siren or merman of the sea. (ILLUSTRATION FROM THE MARVELLOUS ADVENTURES OF ST BRENDAN, 1499)

SANGREAL, or Grail, was the holy vessel of Arthurian mythology during the Middle Ages. It was said to be the cup that Christ drank out of at the Last Supper. It was also believed to have received the blood which flowed from the spear thrust in Christ's side at the Crucifixion. Brought to Britain by JOSEPH OF ARIMATHEA, the rich man who buried Christ, or by his brother-in-law Bron and his son Alan, the Grail was always associated with the early Christian settlement at Glastonbury. Another miraculous object connected with the Grail was a bleeding lance or spear. Sir GALAHAD used its magic power to cure a mysterious ruler, the "Maimed King", who lay between life and death in his castle. It seems, however, that Sir PERCIVAL was originally the knight who saw the Grail, and that it was only in later versions that Galahad took his place as the only knight worthy of such a vision.

The Grail was lost, but it was thought not to have left Britain, rather that it was hidden somewhere in the country because of the

SANGREAL (below) was guarded by angelic women, the Grail Maidens. Here, the dove of heaven bears a gold censer from which arose "a savour as if all the spice of the world had been there", recalling the spicy "greal" of Celtic myth. (THE DAMSEL OF THE SANC GRAIL BY DANTE ROSSETTI, CANVAS, 1874.)

SANGREAL (left), after inspiring the great quest in Britain, was borne back to Sarras by the three good knights, Galahad, Percival and Bors, and was celebrated in a Eucharistic Mass before ascending to heaven. (HOW THE GRAIL ABIDITH IN A FAR COUNTRY BY WILLIAM MORRIS, GLASS, C.1890.)

sinfulness of the times. Indeed, the mere presence of the holy vessel was enough to act as a challenge to most knights to pursue a path of goodness. On its unseen arrival at Camelot, the chivalrous Sir GAWAIN immediately vowed to seek out its home in order to see the Grail for himself. Many of the Knights of the Round Table made similar vows, much to the distress of King ARTHUR, who feared the loss of his best fighting men. But only Sir Galahad successfully completed the quest and died contented. After holding the Grail in his own hands, the young knight's soul was released from his body and "a great multitude of angels bore it up to heaven". That the Grail was the representation of the body and blood of Christ there can be no doubt, for Joseph of Arimathea administered it as part of the sacrament to Sir Galahad, "who had trembled when his mortal flesh beheld spiritual things". It is even stated that Sir Galahad was a descendant of the same Joseph, "the first Christian bishop".

There remains, nevertheless, a powerful charge of Celtic magic in this Christian myth. When "the Holy Grail covered with a white cloth" appeared at Camelot, the vessel filled King Arthur's hall with the most tasty smells, so that the Knights of the Round Table ate and drank as never before. It was, in fact, nothing less than a Celtic cauldron of plenty. When, at the end of the quest, the Grail became "Our Lord's body", the draught that Sir Galahad took from it at Joseph of Arimathea's request ensured his spiritual survival. Like a Celtic cauldron of rebirth, it allowed Sir Galahad to live on in a Christian otherworld. This obvious debt to Celtic mythology meant that the Church never fully embraced the Grail as a Christian symbol. The great popularity of Grail stories forced a degree of toleration, but clerics were always aware of its links with pre-Christian rites. (See also WONDROUS CAULDRONS; HEROIC QUESTS)

SCATHACH (whose name means "shadowy") was a warrior-princess in the Land of Shadows and tutor in the martial arts. One myth recounts that her most famous pupil was the Ulster hero CUCHULAINN. She taught him his famous battle leap and gave him the spear named Gae-Bolg ("Belly-spear"). Although it made a single wound on entry, once inside the body of one of Cuchulainn's enemies, thirty barbs opened to tear the stomach apart. UATHACH, the daughter of Scathach, was Cuchulainn's mistress during his year of training, and was unhappy that he wanted to fight her sister AOIFA. In the event, Cuchulainn was able to defeat Aoifa by trickery and made her his next mistress.

SANGREAL (above) was attained by three very different knights. Galahad, the purest, beheld its contents; Bors, the most worldly, returned to tell the tale; Percival, the simplest, became its guardian. (THE ATTAINMENT BY WILLIAM MORRIS, TAPESTRY, C. 1870.)

SCOTA was said to be the earliest known ancestor of the Scots. According to one version of the myth, she was the daughter of an Egyptian pharaoh. A wise teacher named Niul, who had settled in Egypt, became her husband and they had a child, Goidel, who gave his name to the Gaels. In another tradition, she was the wife of *MILESIUS* and was killed fighting the *TUATHA DE DANANN*.

SEARBHAN, in Irish mythology, was a *FOMORII* warrior, one of the ancient sea gods. This one-eyed, one-armed and one-legged fighter guarded a magic tree, which no one dared approach. However, during the sixteen-year flight of *GRAINNE* and *DIARMUID UA DUIBHNE* from the *FIANNA*, the hard-pressed lovers managed to become friends with Searbhan and he allowed them to shelter in the branches of the magic tree, which made it difficult for *FINN MACCOOL* to find them. However, Searbhan and Diarmuid came to blows when Grainne attempted to eat some of the magic berries that grew on the tree, and the Fomorii warrior was slain.

SETANTA see *CUCHULLAIN*.

SUALTAM MAC ROTH, in Irish mythology, was the brother of *FERGUS MAC ROTH*. An Ulsterman, he accepted *CUCHULAINN* as his own son, although the hero's real father was the sun god *LUGH*. On the night of her wedding to Sualtam Mac Roth, *DECHTIRE* had swallowed a fly and fallen into a deep sleep. In this state she went to the otherworld with Lugh and there conceived Cuchulainn. While Cuchulainn was single-handedly defending Ulster against the invading forces of Queen *MEDB* of Connacht, Sualtam Mac Roth attempted to gather the men of Ulster who had been weakened by *MACHA*'s curse. So desperately did he turn his horse that Sualtam cut off his own head with the sharp edge of his shield. But the severed head continued the call to arms long enough to rouse the warriors.

SEARBHAN (left), the surly one-eyed Fomorii giant, guarded a magic tree, squatting at its foot all day. The eloping lovers, Diarmuid Ua Duibhne and Grainne sheltered in its branches, but Grainne developed a craving for the tree's magic berries. This so enraged the giant that he and Diarmuid fought and the mighty Searbhan was slain with his own club. (ILLUSTRATION ANON.)

SUALTAM MAC ROTH'S (right) head rallied the Ulstermen to battle, even after his death. He had exhorted them in life without success, as they were weakened by Macha's curse. The cries of the severed head at last broke the spell and roused the men to fight. (ILLUSTRATION BY STEPHEN REID, 1910.)

SUIBHNE GEILT, "the mad one", in late Irish mythology was a king cursed by St Ronan. One day King Suibhne was outraged to learn that, without his permission, Ronan was founding a church on his land. Although his wife, Eorann, tried to restrain him, the king rushed to the new foundation, seized the saint's psalter and threw it in a nearby lake. He then laid hands on St Ronan, when a messenger arrived to summon him to an ally's aid on the battlefield. Next day an otter returned the psalter unharmed. St Ronan thanked heaven for this and cursed Suibhne, who assumed the characteristics of a bird, leaping from trees for seven years before his reason returned.

When St Ronan heard about this recovery, he prayed that the king would not return to persecute Christians. So Suibhne was once again on the brink of madness as headless bodies and severed heads harried him. Another priest took pity on the tormented man and wrote down his sad tale, after which Suibhne "died a Christian and his soul ascended to heaven".

TARANIS, "the thunderer", was a Celtic sky god whom the Romans equated with their supreme deity Jupiter. The wheel, which is sometimes used as a symbol of the sun in Celtic art, here represents the electric light of a thunderbolt, symbolized by the trident, a three-pronged spear.
(ILLUSTRATION BY MIRANDA GRAY, 1994.)

TALIESIN was a prophetic bard who was gifted with all-knowing vision, which was symbolized by his shining brow. At the young age of thirteen, he already surpassed all of Arthur's bards in spiritual insight. He is portrayed here as a visionary spirit who was at one with the forces of nature. (ILLUSTRATION BY STUART LITTLEJOHN, 1994.)

TAILTU was the daughter of a ruler of the *FIRBOLG* and wife of Eochaidh Mac Erc, another Firbolg king. She was said to have cleared the forest of Breg so that it became a plain, a task which killed her. Because she was the foster-mother of the sun god *LUGH*, he declared that the festival of Lughnasadh be held in her honour, which took place on the first day of August. It was originally the occasion of a national sporting competition, not unlike the Olympic Games.

TALIESIN ("Shining Brow") was a Welsh wizard and bard and according to Welsh mythology he was the first person to acquire the skill of prophecy. In one version of his story he was the servant of the witch *CERIDWEN* and was named Gwion Bach. Ceridwen prepared a magic brew that, after a year of boiling, was to yield three drops of knowledge. Whoever swallowed these precious drops would know all the secrets of the past, the present and the future. As Gwion Bach was tending the fire beneath the cauldron, some of the hot liquid fell on his finger and he sucked it to relieve the pain (much like *FINN MACCOOL* when he was cooking the Salmon of Knowledge). The furious Ceridwen employed all her magic powers to pursue the boy. During the chase he transformed himself into a hare, a fish and a bird before being eaten by the witch in the form of a grain of wheat. Later Gwion Bach was thrown into the sea and was caught in a fish-trap and renamed Taliesin because of his radiant forehead. "I am old, I am new," he said. "I have been dead, I have been alive." (See also *SAGES AND SEERS*)

TARANIS (whose name means "Thunderer") was one of the few Celtic gods with whom the Romans identified and he was often equated with Jupiter. Monuments to Taranis have been found all over the Celtic world, from the Adriatic coast to the northern regions of Britain. Taranis is usually depicted with his symbol, the wheel. The word "taran" is still used in modern Welsh and Breton to mean thunder.

TEIRNON was lord of Gwent Is Coed and foster-father of *PRYDERI*. Teirnon owned a beautiful mare, and every year on the eve of the first of May the animal gave birth to a foal, which mysteriously disappeared. One year Teirnon decided to keep watch to see what would happen. A giant clawed hand came through the stable window and took the new-born foal. He hacked off the hand but heard a crying coming from outside and found a three-day-old baby boy lying on his doorstep.

Teirnon and his wife took the child in and raised him as one of their own, but as he grew, the resemblance to *PWYLL* became increasingly marked until they knew that he was the missing son of Pwyll and *RHIANNON*.

TEUTATES, also called Toutatis, was one of the Celtic gods mentioned by the Roman historian Lucan and is often equated with the god Mars. His name means "a people" or "a tribe" and so it may well be that the many inscriptions to him are actually dedicated to local deities of a region rather than to a single pan-Celtic figure.

TEIRNON, watching the birth of a foal, was shocked to see a vast hairy arm thrust through the stable window. After hacking at the arm with his sword, Teirnon found a beautiful baby boy in the stable, whom he raised and who turned out to be the lost son of Rhiannon and Pywll, rulers of the realm. (ILLUSTRATION BY ALAN LEE, 1984.)

to Cornwall, where King Mark waited to marry her. The ensuing tale relates the sad course of their love, separation and their deaths. The lovers' end was particularly touching. Having agreed to part, Tristan went to Brittany, but later was gravely wounded and sent for help from Iseult, who had once before cured him of a serious wound. So she sailed to Brittany with a magic cure. It had been agreed that the ship carrying Iseult would hoist a white sail to indicate that she was aboard. However, an incorrect report of a black sail caused Tristan to lose the will to live and he died of his wound. When Iseult was told of her lover's death she too quickly died, but of a broken heart. (See also CELTIC ROMANCE; SINGLE COMBAT)

THOMAS THE RHYMER see *CELTIC OTHERWORLDS*

TRISTAN, the nephew of King MARK of Cornwall, was one of the great lovers of medieval mythology. His name is said to have been given to him after his mother's death in childbirth. Of Breton origin, the story of Tristan and *ISEULT* was popular in Cornwall, Ireland and Brittany. A love potion prepared by Iseult's mother, the Irish queen, was the cause of their great love. Tristan and Iseult drank it accidentally when Tristan was escorting her

TRISTAN and Iseult (left), enchanted by a love potion, gaze at each other in rapture. In one legend, the two had fallen in love before sipping the potion, which only served to quash their scruples. The Victorian design captures the extreme nature of courtly love. (ILLUSTRATION BY EVELYN PAUL, 1900.)

TRISTAN humbly sought the Grail, even though he doubted his chances because of his illicit love for Iseult. At one stage in his quest, he found a splendid castle all alight and alive with song. Sadly, however, he was struck back by a burning beam of light, for only the purest could attain the Grail. (ILLUSTRATION BY EVELYN PAUL, C. 1900.)

TUATHA DE DANANN were "the people of the goddess Dana" in Irish mythology. They were the last generation of gods to rule Ireland before the invasion of the sons of *MILESIUS*, the ancestors of the present-day Irish. The Tuatha De Danann overcame the *FOMORII*, violent and monstrous sea gods, at the second battle of Magh Tuireadh largely because of their superior magic. They were said to have learned magic, crafts and knowledge in four marvellous cities of the north, Falias, Gorias, Finias and Murias. From these cities the Tuatha De Danann brought to Ireland four talismans: the Stone of Fal, which screamed aloud when the rightful king of Ireland placed his foot upon it; the magic sword of *NUADA*, their great war-leader, which was a weapon that could only inflict fatal blows; the spear or

TWRCH TRWYTH (below) was a boar that guarded three treasures between his ears which Culhwch sought to retrieve. Arthur's war-band hunted the boar, and here Mabon, the renowned hunter, skilfully snatches one treasure from between the boar's ears. (ILLUSTRATION BY ALAN LEE, 1984.)

TUATHA DE DANANN (above), an ancient race of Irish gods, went to live underground after their defeat by the Milesians. Beneath grassy mounds, each had his own sparkling sidhe, a subterranean court which glittered with wonders within. (ILLUSTRATION BY ALAN LEE, 1984.)

sling-shot of the sun god *LUGH*, who, as the slayer of *BALOR,* was the bringer of victory over the Fomorii; and the cauldron belonging to *DAGDA,* father of the gods, which was an inexhaustible pot that was capable of satisfying every appetite.

It is clear that the gods known in Ireland as the Tuatha De Danann were common to all Celtic peoples. Their names can be found in Welsh myths and in inscriptions on the continent of Europe. In Ireland they were not entirely lost with the advent of Christianity. Apart from having their exploits recorded by the monks who wrote down the Irish sagas, the Tuatha De Danann took up residence underground as the fairies. On the ancient Celtic feast of Samhain, celebrated on the last day of October to mark the new year, the De Danann were believed to allow mortals to enter their realm.

TUIREANN was the Irish father of three sons who killed Cian, father of the son god *LUGH*. To atone for this crime, Lugh demanded that the sons of Tuireann should perform a series of near impossible tasks, bringing back to Ireland such magical objects as a healing pigskin belonging to a king of Greece and a cooking spit from an undersea kingdom. When fulfilling their final labour they were badly wounded and Tuireann begged Lugh for the pigskin to cure his sons, but the god refused and they died.

TWRCH TRWYTH, in Welsh mythology, was a king who was turned into a gigantic boar for his sins. Between his ears he kept a comb, a pair of scissors and a razor. The retrieval of these objects was one of the hardest of the tasks that the giant Yspaddaden set *CULHWCH* who wanted to marry his daughter *OLWEN*. The boar was an important animal to the Celts and appears in many myths, as well as in statues and carvings. It represented both war and feasting.

UAITHNE *was the god Dagda's inspired harpist. He had three equally gifted sons who played such sad music that on one occasion twelve men died weeping from sorrow. The Celtic bards accompanied their music with lyrics which perpetuated the legends down the generations.* (ILLUSTRATION ANON.)

UATH *submitted three Irish heroes to a beheading contest to test their courage and find the champion of Ireland. The rules allowed a hero to behead the giant but only if he could return the favour on the next day. Only Cuchulainn had the courage to behead the giant and place his head on the block.* (ILLUSTRATION BY JAMES ALEXANDER, 1995.)

UAITHNE, in Irish mythology, was the magic harp of the *TUATHA DE DANANN* god *DAGDA*. It was stolen by the *FOMORII*, the enemies of the De Danann. When Dagda discovered where it was, he called out to the harp to free itself. The harp responded by killing nine Fomorii and then singing Dagda's praises. Uaithne was also the name of Dagda's harpist.

UATH ("Horror") was the name of the water giant who challenged the three Irish heroes *CUCHULAINN*, Laoghaire and *CONALL* to a behead-ing contest. Each was invited to take an axe and chop off the giant's head, provided that he would then lay his own head on the block for the giant to decapitate. Only Cuchulainn rose to the challenge, and was proclaimed by the giant as the Irish champion. After the announcement Uath revealed him-self to be *CU ROI*, the Munster king.

UATHACH was one of the lovers of the great Ulster hero and cham-pion *CUCHULAINN*, and, according to Irish mythology, the daughter of the female warrior *SCATHACH*, who had been Cuchulainn's tutor in the martial arts. When Uathach served

UTHER PENDRAGON, *Arthur's father, hit upon the incredible idea of having a round table at which 150 knights could see each other and sit without quarrelling. Turning to Merlin, he asked him to design a table "round in the likeness of the world".* (ILLUSTRATION ANON.)

the hero food, he forgot his own strength and accidently broke her finger while taking a dish from her hand. Her scream brought her pre-vious lover to Uathach's immediate aid, but Cuchulainn easily slew him in the fight that followed and afterwards Uathach transferred her affection to the victor.

VORTIGERN, *a fifth-century ruler of Britain, tried to build a grand castle, but the walls kept crumbling. The boy Merlin, a precocious seer, was consulted and revealed that two dragons battled beneath the site every night, destroying the castle walls.* (ILLUSTRATION BY ALAN LEE, 1984.)

URIEN, father of *OWAIN*, ruled Rheghed in north-west Britain. His courage and skill as a warrior were celebrated in many songs, includ-ing the work of *TALIESIN*. When the Angles invaded, Urien is said to have fought a successful campaign against them and besieged them on the island of Lindisfarne.

UTHER PENDRAGON (whose name means "dragon head") was *ARTHUR*'s father. According to late-British mythology, Uther was able to sleep with Igraine because he was disguised as her husband, Gorlois, Duke of Cornwall, and the result of their union was Arthur. The wizard *MERLIN* helped in this deception and later Uther killed Gorlois and married Igraine, while Arthur was taken by Merlin.

VORTIGERN was a British ruler who hired Jutish mercenaries, but as increasing numbers of Saxons came into Britain he fled to Wales. Here he tried to build a stronghold, but it kept collapsing. When *MERLIN* was consulted he said that a red dragon (the Saxons) battled with a white dragon (the Britons) beneath the fort and that the red dragon would eventually win.

CELTIC FAMILY TREES

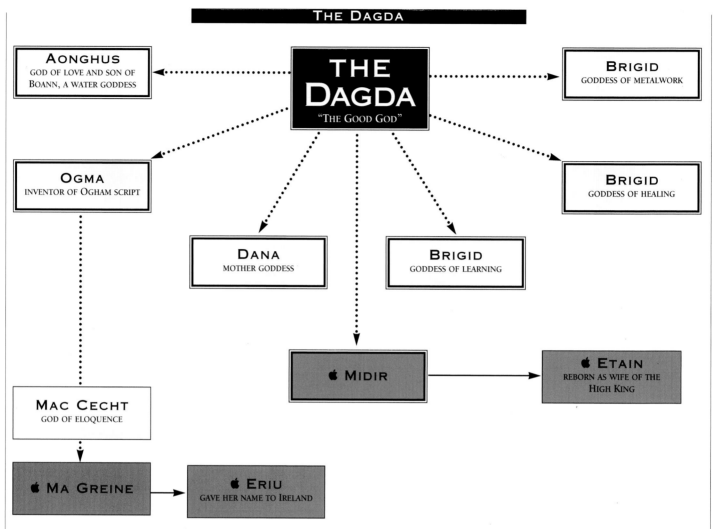

THE DAGDA

AONGHUS
GOD OF LOVE AND SON OF
BOANN, A WATER GODDESS

THE DAGDA
"THE GOOD GOD"

BRIGID
GODDESS OF METALWORK

OGMA
INVENTOR OF OGHAM SCRIPT

BRIGID
GODDESS OF HEALING

DANA
MOTHER GODDESS

BRIGID
GODDESS OF LEARNING

MIDIR

ETAIN
REBORN AS WIFE OF THE
HIGH KING

MAC CECHT
GOD OF ELOQUENCE

MA GREINE

ERIU
GAVE HER NAME TO IRELAND

The Dagda, leader of the Irish Tuatha De
Danann, the gods of Ireland, was a
great warrior usually portrayed as a man
of enormous appetite who owned a cauldron
that could never be emptied. His other
attributes included the club he used as a
weapon, and a magical harp, Uaithne. Much
of the surviving Celtic mythology is vague
about how the gods were related to each
other, but this family tree includes most of the
deities, said at one time or another to be the
children of the Dagda. In the majority of cases
their mothers remain unknown.

DANA, THE GREAT MOTHER GODDESS.

THE ROYAL HOUSE OF ULSTER

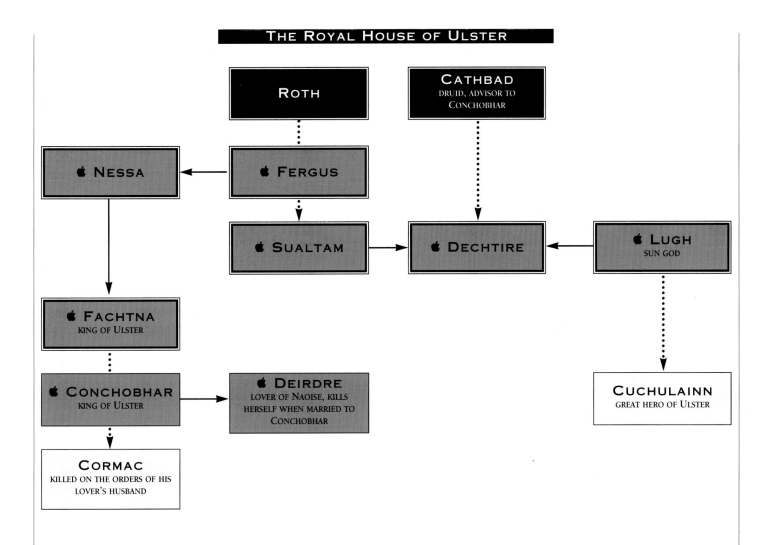

ROTH

CATHBAD
DRUID, ADVISOR TO
CONCHOBHAR

 NESSA

 FERGUS

 SUALTAM

 DECHTIRE

 LUGH
SUN GOD

 FACHTNA
KING OF ULSTER

 CONCHOBHAR
KING OF ULSTER

 DEIRDRE
LOVER OF NAOISE, KILLS
HERSELF WHEN MARRIED TO
CONCHOBHAR

CUCHULAINN
GREAT HERO OF ULSTER

CORMAC
KILLED ON THE ORDERS OF HIS
LOVER'S HUSBAND

CONCHOBAR MAC NESSA AND THE YOUNG CUCHULAINN.

CUCHULAINN IS GUIDED BY HIS FLAMING WHEEL.

Trained for kingship by his ambitious mother, Conchobhar ruled Ulster at the time of the great hero Cuchulainn, who was said to be the grandson of Conchobhar's advisor, the druid Cathbad. Although otherwise a powerful king, Conchobhar's weakness for the beautiful Deirdre led him into a prolonged war. For, having killed Deirdre's lover so that he might marry her, he found his disgusted step-father Fergus siding against him with the enemies of Ulster. Conchobhar finally perished as the result of a magical sling-shot made by Cuchulainn's foster-brother Conall which became embedded in the king's skull.

THE FAMILY OF FINN MACCOOL

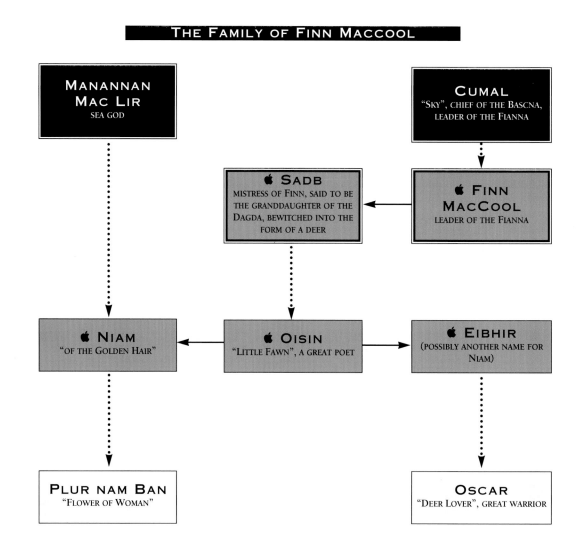

MANANNAN MAC LIR
SEA GOD

CUMAL
"SKY", CHIEF OF THE BASCNA,
LEADER OF THE FIANNA

 SADB
MISTRESS OF FINN, SAID TO BE
THE GRANDDAUGHTER OF THE
DAGDA, BEWITCHED INTO THE
FORM OF A DEER

 FINN MACCOOL
LEADER OF THE FIANNA

 NIAM
"OF THE GOLDEN HAIR"

 OISIN
"LITTLE FAWN", A GREAT POET

 EIBHIR
(POSSIBLY ANOTHER NAME FOR NIAM)

PLUR NAM BAN
"FLOWER OF WOMAN"

OSCAR
"DEER LOVER", GREAT WARRIOR

SADB, A GENTLE GODDESS.

As leader of the Fianna, the warrior bodyguards of the High King of Ireland, Finn can be compared with the British King Arthur. Like Arthur, too, he was believed to lie asleep for ever in a hillside, waiting until his country needs him. His men, who came mostly from the clan Bascna or the clan Morna, were carefully selected for their physical strength and their skill in battle, and they became involved in various adventures throughout the island. Through Finn's relationship with Sadb his story also enters the realm of enchantment, a mythical element reinforced in the tales of his son and grandson.

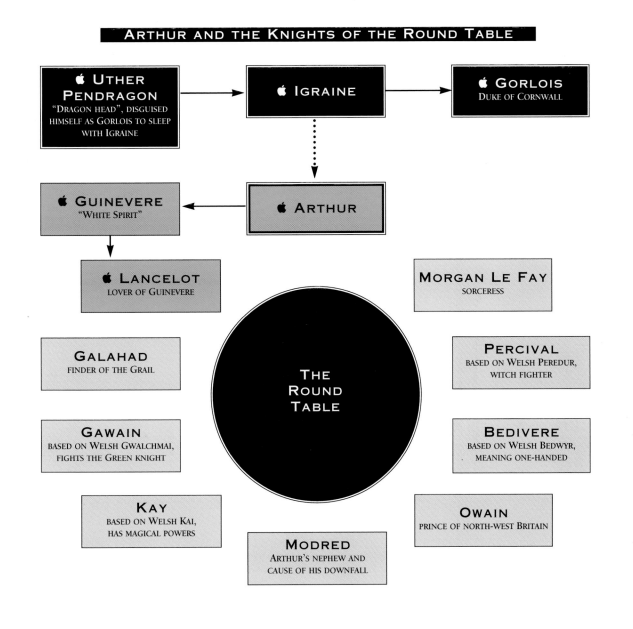

ARTHUR AND THE KNIGHTS OF THE ROUND TABLE

UTHER PENDRAGON
"DRAGON HEAD", DISGUISED HIMSELF AS GORLOIS TO SLEEP WITH IGRAINE

IGRAINE

GORLOIS
DUKE OF CORNWALL

GUINEVERE
"WHITE SPIRIT"

ARTHUR

LANCELOT
LOVER OF GUINEVERE

MORGAN LE FAY
SORCERESS

GALAHAD
FINDER OF THE GRAIL

THE ROUND TABLE

PERCIVAL
BASED ON WELSH PEREDUR, WITCH FIGHTER

GAWAIN
BASED ON WELSH GWALCHMAI, FIGHTS THE GREEN KNIGHT

BEDIVERE
BASED ON WELSH BEDWYR, MEANING ONE-HANDED

KAY
BASED ON WELSH KAI, HAS MAGICAL POWERS

OWAIN
PRINCE OF NORTH-WEST BRITAIN

MODRED
ARTHUR'S NEPHEW AND CAUSE OF HIS DOWNFALL

UTHER PENDRAGON.

The original Arthur of Welsh and Irish tradition was a warrior king whose band of heroes followed him into a variety of adventures. Medieval legend transformed them into courtly knights and altered many of the Celtic ingredients of the old tales for a Christian audience. The magic cauldrons of inspiration and plenty, for example, became the Holy Grail used at the Last Supper. The concept of rebirth survives in Arthur's title of "Once and Future King". The Round Table, too, was a later addition but many of those who sat at it were based on characters found in much earlier stories.

OWAIN AND ARTHUR.

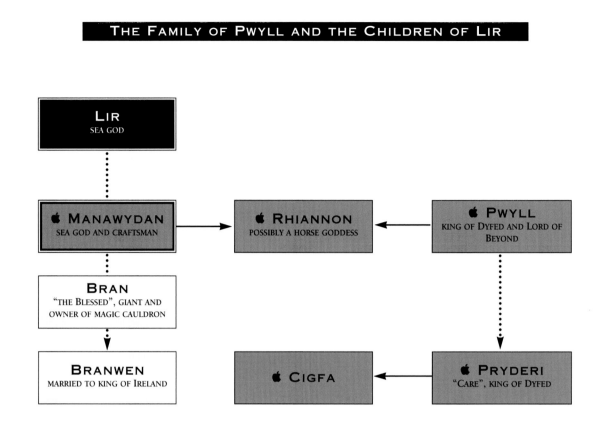

THE FAMILY OF PWYLL AND THE CHILDREN OF LIR

LIR
SEA GOD

 MANAWYDAN
SEA GOD AND CRAFTSMAN

 RHIANNON
POSSIBLY A HORSE GODDESS

 PWYLL
KING OF DYFED AND LORD OF
BEYOND

BRAN
"THE BLESSED", GIANT AND
OWNER OF MAGIC CAULDRON

BRANWEN
MARRIED TO KING OF IRELAND

 CIGFA

 PRYDERI
"CARE", KING OF DYFED

BRAN THE BLESSED, MIGHTY RULER OF BRITAIN.

Common to both Welsh
and Irish mythical
tradition are heroes who
are part mortal and part divine. A
king of Dyfed, Pwyll is also
connected with the otherworld,
both through his own adventures
there and through his wife
Rhiannon, whose magical birds
could wake the dead with their
song. Indeed, Rhiannon's second
husband Manawydan was the son
of the Welsh sea god Lir, whose
other children Bran and Branwen
were similarly seen as humans
with supernatural powers. Later
Celtic writing absorbed these
earlier influences into Arthurian
legend, where Pwyll became
Pelles, keeper of the Holy Grail.

THE CHILDREN OF DON

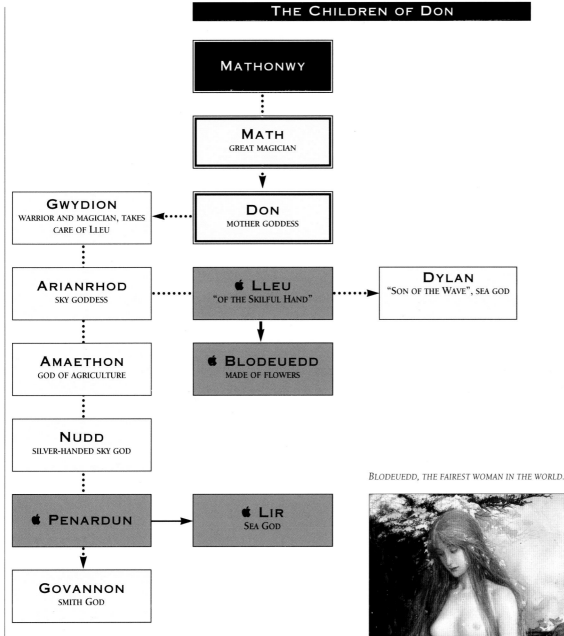

MATHONWY

MATH
GREAT MAGICIAN

GWYDION
WARRIOR AND MAGICIAN, TAKES
CARE OF LLEU

DON
MOTHER GODDESS

ARIANRHOD
SKY GODDESS

🍎 **LLEU**
"OF THE SKILFUL HAND"

DYLAN
"SON OF THE WAVE", SEA GOD

AMAETHON
GOD OF AGRICULTURE

🍎 **BLODEUEDD**
MADE OF FLOWERS

NUDD
SILVER-HANDED SKY GOD

BLODEUEDD, THE FAIREST WOMAN IN THE WORLD.

🍎 **PENARDUN**

🍎 **LIR**
SEA GOD

GOVANNON
SMITH GOD

The Welsh gods can be roughly divided into two groups, The Children of Lir (see opposite) and the Children of Don, the mother goddess. The two groups have been seen by some scholars as representing the forces of light, or the sky, and those of the underworld, though they are linked through Don's daughter Penardun, the wife of Lir. Don herself is the equivalent of the Irish goddess Dana, who gave her name to the Tuatha de Danaan, "the people of the goddess Dana" and the last generation of deities to rule Ireland.

INDEX

PICTURE ACKNOWLEDGEMENTS

The Publishers gratefully acknowledge the following for permission to reproduce the illustrations indicated.

Archiv fur Kunst und Geschichte, London: 9T, 29TL, 30B, 37T, 39BR, 49BL, 49BR, 56L, 64B, 76.
Birmingham Museums and Art Gallery: 17T, 36BR, 51, 67B, 73T, 83T.
The Bodleian Library: 55TL.
The Bridgeman Art Library: 10BR/Phillips Fine Art: 6-7/Lady Lever Art Gallery, Port Sunlight: 10L/Private Collection: 2, 44R/Bibliotheque Nationale:49T/Phillips Fine Art 52B/City of Edinburgh Museums and Art Galleries: 54TR/Private Collection: 57L/Giraudon: 71T.
E. Davison: 35L.
Dundee Art Galleries and Museums: 19T, 20B, 47T, 58BL.
Fine Art Photographic Library: 8, 18T, 19B, 20T, 40BL, 42B, 56R, 82BL.
Glasgow Museums: Art Gallery and Museum, Kelvingrove: 31T.
Yvonne Gilbert: 64ML.
Miranda Gray: 18BL, 44BL, 60T, 62BL, 84B.
King Arthur's Great Halls, Tintagel: 16T, 50TL, 50TR, 53TL, 67TR.
Alan Lee: 21 (all), 22T, 23R, 24R, 27B, 41L, 41BR, 48R, 53TR, 57TR, 57BR, 59T, 61TL, 62T, 63L, 65TL, 65BR, 66TM, 69R, 72 (both), 73BL, 73BR, 74 (all), 75BR, 77 (all), 78 (both), 80L, 81L, 85T, 86 (both), 87BR.
Stuart Littlejohn: 30T, 31BL, 46BR, 84T.
Manchester City Art Galleries: 17B.
Danuta Meyer: 23L, 61B, 80R.
National Galleries of Scotland: 15L, 26, 34B, 38T.
Courtesy Susan Russell Flint: 62BR.
The Tate Gallery, London: 50B.
Courtesy of the Board of Trustees of the Victoria and Albert Museum: 66BL, 82T.

B = bottom, T = top, M = middle, L = left, R = right